APES AND ANGELS

BY THE SAME AUTHOR

THE BALCONINNY

APES AND ANGELS

A BOOK OF ESSAYS

BY

J. B. PRIESTLEY

John Boynton

METHUEN & CO. LTD.
36 ESSEX STREET W.C.
LONDON

First Published	.	.	.	.	*April 19th 1928*
Second Edition	.	.	.	.	*February 1929*
Third Edition	.	.	.	.	*1930*

TO
GERALD BARRY
AND HIS
SATURDAY REVIEWERS

CONTENTS

Apes and Angels

THE FLOWER SHOW

IT is our annual flower, fruit, and vegetable show, and a great event. It may not look to you like a great event—for you can only see two marquees in a field—but you ask Quince, our gardener. He has been thinking and talking about nothing else these past four weeks. You will find him in one of the marquees, looking strangely clean (and somehow smaller) in a new suit. We—that is, Quince and our garden—have won nine prizes, including the first prize for onions. Quince is radiant. He has been after that onion prize from the first, partly because it had been won for seventeen years by the same man, Mr. Snug, who lives near the station, and partly, I suspect, because he must have talked expansively about his onions one night at the 'Duck and Drake' and have been chaffed about them. So he set to work to grow some Ailsa Craigs (for that's our heroine's name) that would smash this seventeen years' record. 'Oi don't care what happens, sur,' he has said to me more than once, 'so long as Oi gets the proize for them thar onions.' He has spent whole days tending them and, latterly, gloating over them. After great deliberation, he chose nine of the largest, made a little stand for them, cutting a hole in the wood for each onion to rest in, so that they made a very fine show indeed, though I must confess that they looked to me like some new garden game, distantly connected with bowls. But there they are now, with the red label on them that dethrones Mr. Snug, who must be content with a blue label and the second prize. Quince cannot keep away from his onions; sometimes he takes a look at the apples (Second Prize) or the tomatoes (Second Prize); but he soon returns to the onions. It is really nothing to him that we had no award for our mixed vegetables (though they were as good as Snug's, which were given a First), that our carrots have not had a look in, that our roses only managed a Third. He has won nine prizes in all, and a First for onions : his ship is in harbour.

Now you can hear the Plumborough Brass Band. They are here in all the bravery of blue and silver uniforms and peaked caps, though it cannot be said they look quite at home in them. There are certain kinds of faces and figures—soldiers and policemen have them— that seem to belong to uniforms, and these honest fellows from Plumborough have not acquired such faces and figures, so look sheepish

The Flower Show

in their blue and silver. Moreover, a brass band should be loud and careless, made up of men who believe that this is the best of all possible worlds and that life can be generously saluted by brazen sounds in waltz time and the clashing of flagons; but the Plumborough Band seems too earnest, thoughtful, scrupulous, and picks out the notes as if it were not certain they ought to be touched, like visitors fingering bric-à-brac. They are telling us now that two for tea and tea for two is their ideal, but they are so uncertain and doubtful that we feel that this view of life is too shallow for Plumborough. We will leave them and visit the man who is dressed in a jockey's cap and silk vest. He is a stout, middle-aged man, and looks ridiculous in this shimmering red and black; and what is more, he is the only man in the field in fancy dress; but he does not care, and has evidently long outgrown self-consciousness. He offers us three darts for twopence—there are prizes for the highest scores of the day—and we all throw darts, and some of them hit the board and some of them do not; but one of us, knowing no more of darts than the rest, makes 107, the highest score of the day so far. Such are darts, and such is life.

We are asked to guess the weight of a pig, and when we go to look at it, we find that it is a mere pigling, no bigger than a fox-terrier. Like most of the pigs in this part of the world,

3

it is mottled, brown and black, and therefore —to my mind—quite unreal. That is probably why I find it impossible to imagine what its weight will be, and anyhow, it is eating all the time, and may be any size before the show is over. We try bowling at skittles, and I do very badly and laugh with the rest, but find myself pointing out that the ground is very uneven and that the bowls themselves are absurdly misshapen. The man we see dodging in and out of the little coal office at the station, a man who looks like a troll, asks us to pay sixpence each and put a stake, with one's name written on it, into a circle of ground where treasure is buried. (This must be a coalman's idea of life.) When we have done this, we are all weighed by the jovial gentleman-farmer in whose field the show is always held. This is something of an ordeal. There is nothing in being weighed if you step on to one of those automatic machines that send a pointer briskly round to a figure on a dial. But when you are weighed by a leisurely human being, who slowly puts one chunk of metal after another into the scale and then carefully announces the final result, it is quite a different matter. I am rather ashamed of my thirteen stone and five pounds, not because I really feel there is anything disgraceful in being a little heavier than most people, but because there is such a thing as the pressure of public opinion, and the world,

The Flower Show

which gets sillier, is now given over to banting and to people made out of cheese-parings after supper. We have a word with the retired schoolmaster who is one of the officials of the show. He is going about putting down names and figures in a notebook, and is quite happy, feeling that he is back again in harness. Schoolmasters never really retire ; there is always, at the back of their minds, an unconquered, never-to-be-surrendered fortress of pedagogy.

We must try the other marquee. The cook, who entered the meat pie and the cake (to cost less than two shillings) competitions, has not won a prize. She did not trouble about the third competition, which is for the best dish of boiled potatoes. They are all here, these dishes, and very unappetizing they look too in the middle of the afternoon—unlike the meat pies and the cakes. You have to be hungry to appreciate a potato, and this is a fact that historians ought to remember. Whenever or wherever the potato is much talked of, hunger is stalking abroad. Opposite the meat pies and the cakes are the exhibits from the school, for the most part pages from copybooks and mats and tiny dolls made of crinkled paper and raffia, the kind of dolls that children prefer to the expensive and eyelashed beauties from the toyshops. On the table that runs down the centre are more fruit and vegetables, and an old man is measuring beans with a piece of string. I am surprised, and rather aggrieved, to discover that George, our giant pumpkin, is here. There is no mistaking him. What he is doing here, I cannot imagine, for there is no prize for which he could compete. Indeed, he serves no common uses, and was grown neither for the kitchen nor the drawing-room. He is to the garden what Falstaff is to the drama of 'Henry IV'. He is its comic poetry, and he has given me more pleasure than any other vegetable or fruit, not excepting those rounded maidens, Rubens creatures, that are the darlings of Quince's heart, the Ailsa Craigs. If ever I visited the kitchen-garden, it was to see George the pumpkin, to mark his ever-increasing girth, to admire his golden and rotund magnificence, to give him an affectionate slap. Can you wonder that such a one figures in a fairy-tale ? Quince must have brought him down here because he felt obscurely that the garden should be also represented by its great comic character. Let us give pumpkin George a farewell slap.

Quince is still in the first marquee, trying—for he is a good modest fellow—not to look too like a man who has broken a long record for the onion prize. But he cannot disguise the fact that he is the happiest man at the show. His father is with him now, a very ancient retired gardener, who looks as if he had grown

out of the earth, like a grand old tree. He
puffs at his short pipe and pretends to philo-
sophic calm, but you can see that he too is
rejoicing over the great onion victory. Quince's
brother is here too, the signalman, very brisk
and natty in a blue serge suit, and seeming to
belong to a later (and perhaps less enduring)
civilization than the other Quinces. He tries
to make fun of the whole thing, this man of
machines, but I know that he was helping
Quince all morning and really has the cause at
heart. The small son and the smaller daughter
of Quince are also here (one got a prize for a
mat and the other for a copybook page—it has
been a great day), and keep pushing their apple
cheeks, which ought to have had prizes too, as
close as they can to their father's sleeve. I am
positive that Quince will not leave this marquee
until the end of the day, that he will be the
last man in it. Here is the scene of his triumphs,
and here he remains. I congratulate him again
on the onion victory. 'They shouldn't ha'
talked at me,' he says ; and I foresee his having
a triumphant pint or two to-night at the
' Duck and Drake ', where they thought he
could not grow Ailsa Craigs. There is nothing
more for us to do now. The fifteen men from
Plumborough are proclaiming, through their
instruments, that they are ' Less than the
du-ust beneath (pom-pom) his chariot whee-
eel', but they do not proclaim it with much

conviction, except the drummer, who is coming into his own in this riot of Oriental passion. As we wander down the road we can still hear him tom-tomming, and we leave the day to him and Quince.

THICK NOTEBOOKS

I WAS killing time in the Broad, Oxford. This is one of the few streets that the go-ahead people of that city seem to have neglected. They will never be able to rival Babbitt's Zenith (and this I take to be their ambition) if they leave streets in the centre of the city lying idle in this way. There is not a single big garage or block of offices or multiple store in the whole length of it, and quite a number of foolish old buildings still cumber the ground there. No wonder the American visitors, pouring in and out of the Mitre, still sneer at the place. Another little spurt of energy, and the Broad, which positively dreams—yes, dreams—now and then in the early morning or at twilight, can be turned into a street fit for go-getters. Look at the High. Years ago, I believe, it was nothing much, just a curving sort of street, the kind you can see in old cathedral cities, but now it looks busy and bright and prosperous, not unlike Hammersmith Broadway, and Mr. Woolworth himself would not despise it. Unfortunately, you cannot kill time in it any longer. If you want to idle, you must sneak up the Turl (which ought to have been widened years ago, and all its little old shops blown up), and lounge into the Broad. I was there, then, the other day, and chanced to remark in the doorway of several bookshops the announcement : ' Thick Notebooks '. Underneath were piles of these notebooks, waiting to be taken into lecture rooms and laboratories and stuffed full of information. The sight of them gave me a little thrill of pleasure. I suddenly realized—to use the phrase that so infuriated Peacock—that my education was finished, that I had no more use for a thick notebook.

I had been free of the schools and the lectures and the set papers for years, but I had forgotten all about it until the thick notebooks reminded me of the fact. Now the taste of liberty was sweet again in my mouth. No longer could masters, angry at being divorced from their pipes, pounce upon me, demanding information of every idiotic kind. Now am I tolerant of and detached from the irregularities of verbs, and there is nobody to be sarcastic at my expense for the amusement of twenty-seven other small boys. What subjunctive is and what pluperfect, I know not, and never a line more shall I write for my ignorance. No longer have I to sit and scribble away, in these same thick notebooks, while be-gowned gentlemen, usually with impediments in their speech and the most absurd mannerisms, make their little

Thick Notebooks

jokes about the policy of Charles the Fifth or the political theory of Hobbes. When I sit and scribble now, it is my own nonsense and not theirs. No longer must I visit quizzical middle-aged dons and read to them, while they fill their pipes with mildest honeydew, essays on subjects that no man ever made amusing. 'For next week, Priestley,' one of them would say, 'you might do a paper on the economic policy of the Netherlands during the seventeenth century. I don't think you'll get any fine writing out of that.' But I always did, always ended with a grand peroration. You see, you don't need to know anything to indulge in fine writing, not the merest ghost of a fact. I was too busy sitting up every night drinking beer with other free spirits and pulling the universe into shape to bother my head about the economic policy of the Netherlands.

Everybody must have noticed that dons are not like other men, that they have a curiously nervous manner, a haunted look, like men who have lost heart's ease and never lie down untroubled at night. Mr. Belloc, who seems to know more about the inner workings of the universe than most of us, once said that they were being punished by God for their intellectual pride. My own account of the matter is different. I think these men are for ever ill at ease because their trade compels them at least once a year to commit a crime, and a peculiarly treacherous crime. Every year the young men come up for the Summer Term, and dream happily through pied April and sweet May, when the lilac and laburnum are heavy over the river, when it is good to hit a ball on the green, to drink beer at open windows, to smoke a pipe at the bookstalls, to go walking at night and hear the sap of life stirring. Never will the blood run more sweetly than it does during those Summer Terms. Then may a man swear eternal friendships, sketch out a new political party or weekly review, fall pleasantly in love with a face he has seen but once. The days are so many sonnets and sonatas.

Then suddenly, on the very rose-crowned threshold of June, a dreadful halt is called. The young men are herded into stuffy rooms, where they must remain morning and afternoon, it may be, for a whole week, staring at blotting paper. We are now about to discover, announce the dons, what you have remembered of your thick notebooks : write it all down on one side of the paper only. And, alas !—the notebooks have been lying these many weeks at the bottom of a mixed heap of textbooks and worn-out tennis shoes and empty tobacco tins. If you are young, and it is May-time, and some of the best fellows in the world (soon, indeed, to be its greatest men) are for ever shouting up at your window to beg your company, you cannot be expected to bother your head about the notebooks. This, then, is the foul trick played annually by the dons, and you may see a sense of their treachery working in their faces.

Not that there are not those who believe in the notebooks. Let every man, woman, and child, they say to us, have plenty of good thick notebooks, and the opportunity to fill them full of facts and theories, and the world is saved. Let us be for ever lecturing and demonstrating and taking notes. If it is a shame that men must work so long and hard, that is because they have so little time and energy for continuing their education. If it is a scandal that men are paid so little, that is because they have not money enough left them for textbooks and laboratory fees and notebooks. Let us look forward to the time when our necessary toil will only occupy us an hour or two, and we can spend the rest of the day educating one another. If men are not wise and good, that is because they have not filled enough notebooks. Find a pile of the thickest notebooks, crammed to the last inch, and you have also discovered one of the wisest and best of men. So runs the creed.

Thick notebooks, however, will never save the world, except that of the manufacturing stationers. There are already too many people solemnly and idiotically taking notes. Most of

them would be better employed looking at
something or thinking over the subject for
themselves. This very week, hundreds of
students of English Literature have begun a
new page by noting that Chaucer's life may be
divided into three periods, or that Cowper,
Burns, and Blake are the heralds of the Romantic
Revolt; and all of them ought to have been
reading something for themselves or trying to
write or finding a job of work to do at home.
Hundreds more, learning history, have set
down page after page of absurdly rationalized
accounts of past events—accounts that turn
every historical personage into a completely
logical creature, when, indeed, they would have
learned more about the making of history if
they had been told to investigate and describe
the latest row in the Tennis Club, for in the
midst of that muddle and brawling they would
have found Clio herself. And notice what a
treacherous subject this is, how insidious its
poison. Before I can begin denouncing education, I have thought of a new way of my own,
and I have but to persist in thinking and
talking about it to find myself facing lecture
rooms snowy with open exercise books, all to
be filled with notes on the new system. There
is no topic that sets more traps for vanity and
egoism. Nearly all the talk we hear about
education is little more than a display of vanity
and egoism : it is Nothing Like Leather all

Thick Notebooks

over again ; the scientists would have us all students of science ; the scholars would turn us into scholars ; the philosophers are positive that we cannot do better than become philosophers ourselves. Nowadays I only prick up my ears when I catch a man recommending a system of education entirely different from the one that knocked him into the particular shape he is. And I rarely do prick up my ears.

I suggest that thick notebooks be abolished. A stationer should be compelled to take out a licence to sell them. A man asking for one should be closely questioned. Is he about to do some original work of his own ? Does he want a notebook to scribble verse in or to sketch comic faces ? If so, well and good. But if he wants to cram the thing with notes of the notes that his lecturer once made of some other lecturer's notes, and all in order that he may compel other unfortunates to fill their thick notebooks in turn, then, I say, he must be driven out of the shop as we—creatures far more innocent and gay—are driven out of public-houses when there strikes the hour at which both our thirst and our sociability lose their official sanction. Let the student buy himself a very thin notebook, inscribe on the first page a sentence or two from Ecclesiastes, listen to his tutors, take a long look at things for himself, and then make a note or two. He may find that he wants ten reams of foolscap, having discovered a world of his own, or he may find that he wants to say nothing at all; but what he certainly will not want is a thick notebook.

T'MATCH

IF you are in Bruddersford on Saturday afternoon, you go to t'match. I was in Bruddersford last Saturday afternoon, and quite automatically set out for t'match. As a matter of fact, there were several football matches, of varying codes, to choose from, and when I marched out of the hotel I had no idea at which particular match I should arrive. I simply followed a grey-green tide of cloth caps, which swept me down streets that grew meaner at every turn, past canals and gas works, until finally we came to the edge of the town. In that part of the West Riding, the Bruddersford district, there is not a very marked difference between town and country. When the last street brings you to a field, you are not aware of any dramatic contrast, simply because the field is not one of your pretty lush meadows, peeping and smiling, but is a dour slab of earth that keeps its grass as short as a wool merchant keeps his hair. This countryside, an angry spur or two of the Pennines, valleys full of black rock, does not regard the local handiwork of man with disfavour. If there must be men about, it says, then let them build factories

and railway sidings and gas works : and so all
these things seem to flower naturally out of
that grim country. There are some parts of
the West Riding that do suggest to you that
industry is the supreme vandal, that the fair
face of Nature has been blackened ; but none
of these fine thoughts come to you in the
neighbourhood of Bruddersford, where it is
obvious that town and country are all of a
piece and the tall black chimneys seem inevitable
if fantastic outcroppings of rock on those steep
hillsides. Moors and mills, smoke and stone :
I need say no more, because either you know
or you don't. (And let us have no talk of the
Brontës, who did not live in this particular
district, who were not Yorkshire people, and
who should be given a close season.) It is a
country, whether it expresses itself in fields or
streets, moors or mills, that puts man on his
mettle. It defies him to live there, and so it
has bred a special race that can live there,
stocky men with short upper lips and jutting
long chins, men who roll a little in their walk
and carry their heads stiffly, twelve stone of
combative instinct. If you have never seen
any of these men, take a look at the Yorkshire cricket team next summer. Or come to
t'match.

I paid my shilling and then discovered that
it was a rugger match, presumably the Northern
Union, the professional, thirteen-a-side, all

T'match

scrimmage game. I was annoyed to find that the match had started. There were about ten thousand people there, including a thousand little boys all screaming in a special pen, but I was disappointed at the lack of enthusiasm. Nobody apart from the boys seemed to be paying much attention to the game. I noticed too that the players, though sufficiently well-built fellows, were not the giants I expected to find in Northern Union rugger. It was all very disappointing. 'Who are they?' I asked the man on my right. 'Nay, ah doan't knaw,' he replied. 'It's t'lads' match. Under twenty-one.' I began to see light. 'This isn't the proper match, then?' I remarked to him. He stared at me: 'This is nowt,' he said, dis-passionately. 'T'match begins in a minute or two Bruddersford versus Millsbury.' This explained everything: the afternoon had not yet begun.

I cast a complacent eye on t'lads, who very soon cleared off to the sound of an odd cheer or two. Then there was silence. We all waited for Bruddersford and Millsbury to appear. I could feel a difference in the atmosphere. Then they came running on and we all shouted. Bruddersford were in red, and Millsbury were in blue. The forwards on both sides were colossal fellows, fit to engage in a scrum with a few elephants. A minute later t'match had begun. The Bruddersford back immediately performed several miracles, and

19

we all applauded him and called him Joe.
'That's right, Joe!' we told him, though I
cannot say he took much notice of us. Then
Number Eight of Millsbury, who looked like a
bull in a blue jersey, grabbed hold of Joe a
minute or two after he had rid himself of the
ball and threw him several yards. Joe did not
seem to care very much, but we were very
angry. 'Mark him, Joe!' we cried: 'Watch
Number Eight, Joe!' These tactics, however,
could not prevent Bruddersford from scoring.
Ginger began it. There is always a red-haired
man in every team—or if there is not, then the
manager does not know his business—and this
one was a little wiry fellow, who played three-
quarter. (At least, he was always waiting
outside the scrums to pick up the ball, and
frequently one saw him emerging from a heap
of humanity, looking none the worse for having
had about half a ton of bone and muscle
piled on him.) Suddenly, then, Ginger went
through like a little red shuttle, and we all
shouted away as the ball sailed between the tall
posts a minute afterwards. Then the game was
lost for half an hour in a desert of scrimmages.
There are too many scrimmages in this Northern
Union game. I got tired of seeing those twelve
men pushing and heaving.

The man on my left, whose cap was too small
and moustache too large, was disgusted. 'Nay,
Bruddersford,' he kept shouting in my ear,

T'match

'lake foitball.' He was angry, passionate, a man with shattered ideals. He had come to see foitball laked and it was not being laked properly. Bruddersford were winning, but being something more than a mere partisan, being a critic of the art, he was not comforted. 'They're not passing, not passing,' he told my left ear-drum. 'Look at that! Nay, Bruddersford!' he would cry. He appeared to suspect that my left ear-drum entertained views of the game quite different from his own. Just before half-time, a man in front of me but some distance away, a man with a cap at the back of his head, a red muffler, and an angry unshaven face, above which he tilted a beer bottle from time to time, suddenly created a diversion. He was, I think, a Millsbury supporter, one of those men who have no money but yet contrive to follow their football teams wherever they go, and he must have entered into an argument with some Bruddersford enthusiast. I do not know what they were arguing about; all that I do know is that suddenly this man turned round to face us and cried at the top of his voice: 'Neck and ankles, that's what I say. Neck and ankles.' He seemed to be in a towering rage. Then he turned round again to look at the game, but a moment later, still more furious, he cried to us his mysterious slogan: 'Neck and ankles!' Then he added, as an afterthought: 'You can't get away from it. Neck and ankles ! He took another long pull at his bottle. ' Ger aht wi' yer ! ' we said to him. This roused him to a frenzy, and putting down his bottle and raising his voice, he yelled : ' B——y neck and ankles ! B——y neck and b——y ankles ! ' And he glared defiance at some three thousand of us. ' Put a sock in it ! ' we yelled back to him, and turned our attention to the game.

The two great events of the second half were Nosey's try and the sending off of Millsbury's Number Six. Nosey had done very little up to the time he received that pass, and I had come to the conclusion that he was not a man worth watching. He got the ball, however, well in his own half, and began to race at a prodigious speed down the touchline. Millsbury made a rush at him, but, after he had pushed away one or two and swerved from two or three more, he gathered speed and simply outran all the others, curving in exquisitely at the last to plant the ball neatly between the posts. You should have heard our shouts for Nosey. Even the critic on my left was impressed, and was very satirical at the expense of some unknown detractors of the great Nosey. ' And then they say 'e can't run. Can't run ! ' he sneered. ' Beat 'em all. Beat 'em all.' He liked this phrase so much that he kept repeating it at odd moments during the next quarter of an hour.

T'match

But he was not so repetitious as the little man in the macintosh behind me. It was the sending off of Millsbury's Number Six that set him going. This Number Six had completely lost his temper and made a rush at a Bruddersford man when the ball was far away. The Bruddersford man contrived to throw him down, but the referee determined to make an example of this Number Six—for the play was becoming very rough—and so ordered him off the field. We gave him a boo or two as he left. But the little man in the macintosh was still indignant, and proclaimed, in those flat tones that are sometimes discovered in fanatics, that if he, Number Six, had tried it on with Mulligan (the burliest of all the Bruddersfords) Number Six would not have walked off but would have had to have been carried off. The game began again, and blues and reds charged one another and fell in heaps. 'If 'e'd tried it on with Mulligan, 'e'd 'ave been carried off,' came the flat voice from behind. Another try for Bruddersford: Ginger again! But Joe couldn't convert it. Hard lines, Joe! 'If 'e'd tried it on with Mulligan '—yet once more. The blues are tiring now, and they are bad-tempered, but we are giving them as good as we get. Nearly time, now. Another try? No. Time. We give them a cheer. 'If 'e'd tried it on with Mulligan '—but no, we must get out. The little man with the macintosh, we feel, will be the last spectator to leave the ground. He will tell the man who closes the gates what would have happened if Number Six had tried it on with Mulligan. The rest of us are out now, swarming down the narrow road, towards the trams. We are all talkative, amiable, relaxed : our combative instincts put to bed for a little space. We can turn a more gentle regard upon the gloomy hills, the factories and gas works and railway sidings ; for the time being they do not trouble us ; we have been to t'match.

OTHER PEOPLE'S ACCOMPLISHMENTS

I WAS early for dinner and there was nobody in the drawing-room to talk to, so I switched on the wireless. I like the wireless: it has made life even more fantastic and ridiculous than it was before. How delightfully absurd it is to walk into your drawing-room in Shropshire and to know that all your family there, listening-in, have their ears in the Albert Hall or the Winter Garden Pavilion, Bournemouth! How amusing it is to touch a switch and then find that an earnest little man is at your elbow talking to you about bowls in the coming season or home life in Baluchistan, and what a comfort it is to be able to switch him off again, to extinguish him with a breath, as it were, without even hurting his feelings! Well, I switched on the wireless and found myself being addressed by a very thin and precise voice. Apparently I had blundered into an eulogy of some great man, whose name I never heard. I gathered that his explorations were famous. Then the voice went on: 'He was no mean botanist, and was a fine geologist. The Astronomer Royal admitted that he owed him a great deal.' I did not wait to hear any

3

25

more. I switched off. That was something I could do; I, who am neither geologist nor botanist, astronomer nor explorer, I could switch off, and I did. What I heard was sufficiently depressing, and I did not want to be told, as I feel sure I should have been told, that this great unknown could speak twelve languages, had won the mile and the amateur lightweight championship, and had played for England at hockey, and was, of course, an excellent musician. I had had enough. I sat in silence until dinner was ready, brooding. Then I went and ate heartily. I nearly always do, but you can't make much of an accomplishment out of that. If my turn ever came to be eulogized (and I see no reason why it ever should), they would not be able to hide the great blank spaces by remarking : ' He was always a hearty feeder.'

This matter of other people's learning and accomplishments has been worrying me for some time. I never read the life of any important person without discovering that he knew more and could do more than I could ever hope to know or to do in half a dozen lifetimes. To begin with, unless these people chance to be obvious invalids, like Stevenson or Tchekhov, they are always tremendous athletes, with surprising strength, powers of endurance, and so forth. They could all walk and run and climb our heads off, even when they were

Other People's Accomplishments

seventy. Then they all have the gift of tongues. You never catch a glimpse of them sitting down to learn a new language, not even running an eye over its irregular verbs, yet it is admitted that they speak any number with an astonishing fluency and purity of accent. They never confine themselves to one science, but are inevitably masters of several. The big book of Nature they know by heart. Only the other day I was reading an account of a great novelist, a most sophisticated and subtle person, and was told that he knew the name and habits and history of every wild flower and plant and tree and bird in the country. Nor is that all. There is not one of these big-wigs who is not (I quote the customary phrases) a sensitive and accomplished musician, or an extraordinary fine amateur water-colourist, or the possessor of a magnificent prose style. We are always told that had circumstances been different, their talents were such that they need only have given their serious attention to one or other of these arts to have procured for themselves lasting and perhaps world-wide reputations. So runs the legend of the eulogists.

I am baffled. How is it done ? I ask the question again, and my voice rises to a scream of envy and vexation. Consider what is involved in this matter (so lightly touched upon and dismissed) of music or water-colour painting or fine writing, what years of serious application, of drudgery at the keyboard, the easel, or the writing-desk. It is one thing to strum on the piano, as you and I do, faking the left-hand passages as we go along, or to daub a few patchy water-colours, or to paste on to clumsy prose some old spangles of rhetoric, and it is quite another thing to be an accomplished musician or artist or writer. If the first were meant, I could understand it; but the second—and as a mere recreation, too! And then to add the athleticism, the sciences, the tongues, the natural history! I am bewildered and crushed. The very idle rumour of fellow-creatures so wonderfully gifted makes me dwindle in my own estimation to the size of a gnat. I cannot but be thankful that I never meet any of them. Who can be surprised when their biographers (at least until the malice of time conjures forth its Stracheys and Guedallas) doff hats and lower voices throughout the length of two big volumes? But in all this there is no comforting word, no single glance of encouragement, for us ordinary mortals, whose years seem to be passed in a very different world, in which there is time to do so very little, and there is so much sad erosion in its tides that we count ourselves fortunate if we can retain our grasp and knowledge of a little trick or two that we have made our own.

When I put myself in imagination by the side

Other People's Accomplishments

of these giant Crichtons, I seem to be as idle and ignorant as a Hottentot. I know that it is the fashion among men who write essays to pretend to be more idle and ignorant than they really are. Lamb began it (see his essay, ' The Old and the New Schoolmaster '), and now the pretence has become part of a tradition. Well, I will have none of it. Here there is no such humorous pretending. I do not want to be thought indolent and unaccomplished. I should like to be able to do all manner of things— to navigate a ship, to play the clarionet, to make beautiful long speeches in public, to act Hamlet and Falstaff on succeeding nights, to shape an arm-chair. I should like to know all about molecules and high finance and forestry in Burma and Elizabethan music and comets and the Lesser Antilles and peewits and tropical diseases and English water-colours and the American Civil War. But the fact remains that I do not see any possibility of my ever becoming really learned and accomplished. There seems to be no time, or time only to forget what once I knew, for my store gradually decreases. Thus I have now no knowledge whatever of the sciences, in which I once received a thorough if rudimentary instruction. It must be understood that I am not boasting of my ignorance, like some superior Classics man : I am ashamed of it, yet I cannot see that the fault is mine. It has just occurred

to me that I once knew German and read
Goethe and Heine. Now I doubt if I could
ask for a bed or a cigar in that tongue. I have
forgotten nearly all the history and philosophy
I once knew (and I made these subjects my
special study at one time) ; but perhaps that is
no great matter, for they have probably had all
the effect required of them in humanizing such
intellect as I possess. I never knew anything
about Nature, flowers and birds and trees and
so forth, and if I lived to be a thousand I could
never become one of those persons who can tell
you what anything is at a glance. There is
actually some slight gain here, though, because
I do contrive to learn the names of about three
flowers and birds every year, though I am never
very certain of them. But what is such a tiny
gain when compared with my immense losses !

I believe I write a little better than I used
to do, and my bridge has recently improved.
The rest is a melancholy tale of time's depreda-
tions. I learn little or nothing new and forget
what knowledge I once possessed. My accomplishments are rusted, mildewed, faded, tattered :
my piano-playing is gone ; I cannot dance now
nor play football ; my billiards and chess are
contemptible ; I could draw a little once, but
that too has gone ; even my French is vile, and
I puff and pant, grow fat, and creep about in
the shadow of a liver. If we were all in the
same boat I would be consoled, but obviously

Other People's Accomplishments

we are not. There are all these important persons, who know everything, who can do everything. I should be comforted if I read notices of them that ran : 'He knew more about atoms (or foreign policy or sun-spots or kidney diseases or violet rays) than any other man of his time, but in all other respects he was little better than an ignorant buffoon, holding ridiculous political and social views, and being without any accomplishments, any sense of music, art, literature, or any mental or physical graces.' But we never meet with any such statements. Sometimes I am reckless enough to fancy that these long lists of accomplishments are not strictly accurate, that exaggeration has crept in somehow. Unfortunately, however, I am rarely in a position to test them. But now and again I am told that certain politicians, famous examples of your astonishingly brilliant all-round men, have among other accomplishments the ability to write a fine prose style. And so I have taken the trouble to read some of the things they have written, these casual great stylists, and what I have read has made me wonder. Have the other things, the knowledge of the sciences, the natural history, the athletic feats, the music and the water-colours, been appraised in the same queer fashion ? No doubt there is envy behind this suspicion, but still—I wonder.

THE PORT

THIS morning I went down to the docks
with my friend, the marine surveyor. He
had a ship, now in dry dock, to look over, the
first for many weeks. There have been very
few ships, whole or damaged, in this port these
many months, and as we walked down towards
the docks, my friend talked of old days that
would never return with any tide. A vast fleet
had sailed away from this port for ever. My
friend is not young and, like all his kind, an
admirable kind, he turns no rosy spectacles on
the future. He is not sentimental about the
past and, like all the men I have ever met who
have had to do with the sea, he cannot be
sentimental about the future. He has the usual
close conservative grain of his type, and possibly
he exaggerates the evils of to-day and the peril
of to-morrow, but it was impossible, keeping
step with him and following his pointing finger,
not to feel that something was passing from
these seas. He kept lightly and realistically
to the facts, the actual substance of the scene
around us, and it was left for me, romantic,
sentimental, literary, to make what I would
of it. Perhaps the morning artfully evoked

The Port

the mood. It was bright enough, a good day for late November, with a sun to see and feel, faintly caressing your shoulders. But it was all so quiet, so dim. There was mist trailing through the town, and a white fog down the Channel. Beneath the bright upper air, the distant things were the merest wraiths and everything close at hand was hushed and faintly shining, a place in a dream. Now and then, but so rarely as to be startling, a siren would suddenly shatter the silence, coming from nowhere and leaving behind only a deeper quiet in which there was a faint irony, an irony of ghosts. Some one was calling the roll of ships, it seemed, and only these were answering.

We passed through the notorious quarter where the seamen's lodgings are, and as we walked along my friend told me stories about the place. He told them with that unconscious air of pride which very respectable citizens cannot escape if they describe to you the depravity of their city. This morning, however, the quarter looked innocent enough, merely so many streets of dingy little houses, with an outlandish name, an Ahmed or Chung Soo, here and there, an occasional vague Lascar or heavily muffled negro standing at a corner, and some half-caste women cleaning their doorsteps. It seemed curiously vacant, lifeless. Perhaps most of them were asleep, though the morning was wearing away. Perhaps there were only a handful of sailors in all these lodging-houses, and Ahmed and the rest were still waiting for company. It looked as if some of them would have to wait for ever. Yet when we came out, passed the chandlers' and gaudy tobacconists' shops, and arrived at the dingy Board of Trade offices, there seemed to be people enough. The square there, muddy and raw, was filled with idlers, standing about in little groups and hardly making a movement. They were listless, drab, silent. They watched the heavy groaning tram creep jerkily up to the square. I had a feeling that they were all waiting for something to happen and yet knew that nothing would happen. What vile places these ports would be if it were not for the fact that they are on the very border of magic ! Somewhere beyond this dreary tangle of railway lines and little bridges and sheds is radiant fantasy, emerald water and great scarlet birds, a glimpse of Pernambuco or Yucatan. You go this way, where our grime seems thickest, cross your last plank, and when next you tread on land, the cockatoos are screaming round you and a black man is slashing at a green coco-nut so that you may slake your thirst. As exits these ports are endurable, but what foul entrances they must make ! Who, coming from the sea to England, would imagine that they too lead back to a fantasy, lovelier and more subtle, the witchery of meadow and hawthorn that is ours ?

The Port

We made our way to the dry dock where my companion had to inspect his ship. She was from Ireland and had ripped some of her plates on the way over. There she was, high and dry, with a little army of pygmies tinkering at her. Here indeed was a most heartening noise and bustle. We had collected one or two marine superintendents and other persons of importance in the dock world, big solid men, much given to shaking hands and addressing people by name : ' What d'you think, Cap'n Brown ? ' ' That's so, isn't it, Mr. Smith ? ' In third-rate stories about the sea, the personages are always rather wild and picturesque, like bad artists, but I have frequently noticed that in real life, as in really good fiction, the men of the sea, skippers and engineers and pilots and the like, are always very solid and punctilious and respectable men, typical members of what some fools are always calling the ' bourgeoisie ', who may have done many wild and desperate things but whose dream of life is a spell with the missis in a little suburban villa, a tiny greenhouse, and a walk down the main street, dressed in a good dark suit and a bowler hat, exchanging greetings here and there : ' Morning, Cap'n Brown ! ' ' Morning, Mr. Smith ! '

It was odd to tread the decks of a ship and look down to see no water but a dry floor and a host of men at work there, to smell the carbide from the acetylene welders below and to hear such a clanging and hammering that it seemed as if the whole ship were being knocked to pieces. It was odd, too, to go down there and watch the goggled men directing their awful flames and turning iron rivets into so many showers of sparks and liquid golden drops of metal, to look up at the vast curving hull of the ship and at the vast bronze propeller, now forlorn in mid-air. What a good solid job of work this mending of ships is, making most of our tasks seem mere hocus-pocus! I had left my companion with the chief officer (who looked exactly like Little Tich—taller certainly, but with the same face and figure—so that I expected him at any moment to break into song and dance), but after I had wandered round the ship and descended to the floor of the dock, their conference and tour ended. My friend joined me again, and told me all about plates being ripped, wood being spired into mere pulp by the sea-worm, ships that were down thirty fathom just off Lundy, all plain facts—for he is crammed with facts about everything—but to me as romantic as an Arabian Night. By this time we had left the dry dock behind; the noise of hammering had utterly vanished; and again there was silence. Here and there a ship showed itself through the light mist that covered the docks, but the great basins, faintly shining, dream-like, seemed

The Port

sadly vacant. Not long ago, I was told, all those docks were crowded with shipping, were a maze of derricks and smoke-stacks, but now not only was there room enough and to spare, but there was desolating vacancy. The rails were empty of trains, and we could stroll at ease over all the bridges, their 'Keep to the Left' notices being now simply farcical. There was no traffic over them. No lorries came clattering through, no crowds of men rushed over them towards the town or the waiting boats. The great cranes or chutes were all motionless, as if they forlornly sniffed the raw, empty air, monsters awaiting a prey that never came. We left the docks, passed once more through the little square where the Board of Trade and the idlers stared at one another, and came at last to a great block of shipping offices, the tallest building in the neighbourhood. 'I'll take you up to the roof,' my companion said, pointing the way to the lift. 'You get a good view up there.' It was a flat roof, high above the surrounding chimney-pots, boasting of nothing but a tiny greenhouse, where the caretaker had his aerial garden. But beyond the immediate tangle of roofs and gloom of narrow streets, there was nothing to be seen. The hills were completely lost in the thickening mist. Not a glimmer of the Channel came through the fog. The docks were fading out, and the nearest were only the faintest shadow.

Apes and Angels

'You've been unlucky,' I was told, 'for any kind of clear day would have shown us everything.' I promised that I would return and see it all. I hope I shall see it all: the Channel shining and brave with shipping; the docks alive with moving derricks; the air resounding with sirens and locomotive whistles and the shouts of busy men. But I could not help wondering whether I ever should, whether something had not gone for ever. I remember a solitary hooting, like a knell, as we quitted the roof, and how cheerful the smoking café seemed, with its smell of hot coffee, its tobacco smoke, its clatter of tongues and dominoes. There we had a good talk about the East India Company.

THE TWO-AND-FOURPENNY
FAIRYLAND

THE papers tell us that there is a boom in musical comedy. I can believe it, for, being in town the other evening, I saw longer theatre queues than I have noticed for years, and most of them were attached to the Princess This or the Lady That. For every revue we have at present, I believe, at least four musical comedies. Now that seems very extraordinary, if only because you and I prefer revue as a light entertainment to musical comedy. It achieves wit and humour with greater frequency and ease, and offers us far less silly and tedious stuff. It is a sophisticated entertainment, and you and I (but especially you) are sophisticated persons. We are teased or bored by the musical comedy's pretence of having a plot. We do not care a rap whether the Princess marries the Captain of Dragoons or not, whether the millionaire yachtsman and the beautiful shopgirl will meet again or have parted for ever, and we are only maddened by the ever-recurring appeals of these lovers in three-four time. We have no more interest in their personal relations than we have in those of butterflies. Not for

one moment do we imagine that we are looking
at a princess or a shopgirl, for the figure before
us is obviously that of Miss Treacly Sweet, and
we are ungallant enough to admit that we care
nothing for that bright and sugary young lady.
The writ of these musical comedy queens does
not run among us. But the ladies of revue,
the Lillies and the Lawrences and the Gays,
are a very different matter. There is, I maintain, more of the acid spirit of the age in Miss
Beatrice Lillie's performance of a sentimental
song (sung slightly out of tune and with many
a catch in the breath) than there is in the
complete works of Mr. Noel Coward.

No, if we visit musical comedy at all, it is
simply to renew our acquaintance with the
comedians, those dynamos of drollery and
character, perhaps the most massive personalities the English Stage can show. There is
a sound and full-bodied pleasure in the thought
that the Chancellor is going to be Mr. George
Graves, that the young man who will bring the
parcel to the house will be Mr. Leslie Henson,
that the commercial traveller, now ringing the
bell, is none other than Mr. W. H. Berry and
that the sight of so many pretty girls will
immediately go to his head. These are, we
will admit, very droll cards and trumps all.
Nevertheless we have found that they cannot
always win the rubber of an evening's entertainment. Here—to change the metaphor—are

oases indeed, but in order to reach them we are compelled to travel across deserts of stupid plotting, cheap sentiment, and damnable iteration in song. So we stay at home. But vast numbers of our fellow-citizens, more particularly daughters of our fellow-citizens, do not stay at home, but fill every theatre, even Old Drury itself, where musical comedy is being played. What is the secret of its attraction? What is the explanation of those long lines of patient folk with their moist and warm two-and-fourpences in their hands? What's Princess This or Lady That to them? The dramatic critics, those weary, cynical men, could tell us, I have no doubt, but while they are drip-dripping the vitriol into a phrase or two, I will take leave to advance a theory of my own. It is this, that what these audiences, more especially the poorer members of them, the patient and loyal one-and-tens and two-and-fours, really like in musical comedy are precisely those things that most of us dislike in it, namely, the plots, the setting, the atmosphere. By waiting at a door in Shaftesbury Avenue and then climbing some stairs, they are able to escape from this real world into an ideal one. Princess This or Lady That is to them what Plato's Republic is to an idealist philosopher.

That the musical comedy presents us with a world of its own will be allowed by every one who has seen half a dozen of these things. It

41

4

Apes and Angels

is always the same world, and so long as it creates illusion (which, of course, it doesn't to sophisticated persons), it provides an admirable means of escape from the real world, which is, it must be remembered, a very grimy workaday affair for most of these two-and-fourpennies. Let us consider this other world of musical comedy. To begin with, it does away at one stroke with all the evils and limitations of our own world. It is almost timeless : its sun, moon and stars are outside mutability. It has banished death, disease, poverty, dirt. It knows neither grey days nor rainy nights, but is bathed for ever in bright sunlight or softest purple moonlight. Arcadia itself could never boast better weather. I have never seen a map of this curious world, though I know that it has its own London, New York, Paris, a vague Central Europe, a Far East and South Sea Islands ; but wherever we travel in it, all the places are alike in being bright and gaily-coloured and brand-new. Everywhere there are bluer skies, greener leaves, and brighter electric lights than even Monte Carlo can show. Sea travel there is an affair of sunlit shining decks and an exquisitely calm blue ocean, and there is never a hint of tumbling grey seas and the smell of oil and bilge-water and sea-sickness and fog. Is it surprising then that so many people should see in it an ideal world ? Yet we have hardly begun to catalogue its charms.

Two-and-Fourpenny Fairyland

It is a world of faultless new clothes. What more could be desired by the heart of a girl, compelled as she probably is to wear that old thing she had last year unless something wonderful turns up at fifteen-and-nine ? Even its very rags (a disguise, of course) are new and straight from Savile Row. To wear clothes and frequently change them is the chief occupation of the inhabitants of this world. For the rest there is singing and dancing and flirting and, to crown all, true love that will never die. There is no work of any kind. As a rule it shows us places where work has never even been heard of, but even such places as large stores in this world do not conduct any business but are given up to revelry. This is perhaps as well, because both the owner and his manager are obviously men who exist to make jokes, and all the staff are very pretty girls all about the same height and most inconveniently dressed for business. But we know that they will not have to pretend that they are in business long. Here nobody is tied down to one dreary job. There is travel and fun for everybody. This is chiefly due to the amazing hospitality that is offered here. It is nothing to find fifty people, indeed all the people who happen to be present, accepting an invitation to go at once from London to Tahiti. They cry ' Hooray ! ' and well they might. Nobody is ever left out of an invitation, or if they are,

it does not matter because they always find
their way across the seas and turn up, probably
with a new song and dance. After this, can
anybody deny that this is a charming world ?
What fun it would be if we could travel in this
fashion, without any trouble and for ever
remaining spick-and-span, strutting in eternal
sunshine, and know that nobody was being left
out, that we were not enjoying ourselves at the
expense of our fellows !

All the women in this world are young and
pretty and very gay, and if at any time they
do feel miserable they are able to relieve their
feelings in a song in waltz time. They are
never misunderstood for more than a couple of
hours at the most. They always marry either
a prince or a millionaire, and their weddings are
a blaze of glory, something for a girl to dream
about. The men are just what men ought to
be, that is, they are either very funny—real
comics who would make you nearly die of
laughing, they would—or they are young and
tall and handsome and wonderfully groomed,
and the possessors of noble baritone voices,
with which they do their wooing. And she's
so pretty and he's so handsome, and they love
one another so passionately that it fair gives
you a thrill and a funny little ache to look at
them and listen to them. And behind them is
the whole bright world of new clothes and jokes
and travel and riches and eternal summer, with

Two-and-Fourpenny Fairyland

never a sight or a word of work and illness and
rainy days and shabby old clothes and pimples
and cold mutton and snarling shop-walkers
and grumbling foremen and crowded buses and
long Sunday afternoons in bed-sitting rooms.
You have only to save up one-and-ten or
two-and-four, take a bus or tube, and wait for
an hour or two, and then at last a door will be
opened and you will climb the stairs and settle
into a seat. Once there you travel farther than
you have ever travelled before, as far indeed
as ever man can travel, for you will soon take
leave of this real world and find yourself in an
ideal one. And that, I suggest, is the secret of
musical comedy and those long waiting queues
and crowded theatres. It is also, of course, the
secret of many other things.

FIRST SNOW

MR. ROBERT LYND once remarked of Jane Austen's characters: 'They are people in whose lives a slight fall of snow is an event.' Even at the risk of appearing to this witty and genial critic as another Mr. Woodhouse, I must insist that last night's fall of snow here was an event. I was nearly as excited about it this morning as the children, whom I found all peering through the nursery window at the magic outside and chattering as excitedly as if Christmas had suddenly come round again. The fact is, however, that the snow was as strange and enchanting to me as it was to them. It is the first fall we have had here this winter, and last year I was out of the country, broiling in the tropics, during the snowy season, so that it really does seem an age since I saw the ground so fantastically carpeted. It was while I was away last year that I met the three young girls from British Guiana who had just returned from their first visit to England. The two things that had impressed them most were the endless crowds of people in the London streets, all strangers (they emphasized this, for they had spent all

First Snow

their lives in a little town where everybody knew everybody,) and the snow-covered landscape they awoke to one morning when they were staying somewhere in Somerset. They were so thrilled and delighted that they flung away any pretence of being demure young ladies and rushed out of the house to run to and fro across the glittering white expanses, happily scattering footmarks on the untrodden surface, just as the children did in the garden this morning.

The first fall of snow is not only an event but it is a magical event. You go to bed in one kind of world and wake up to find yourself in another quite different, and if this is not enchantment, then where is it to be found ? The very stealth, the eerie quietness, of the thing makes it more magical. If all the snow fell at once in one shattering crash, awakening us in the middle of the night, the event would be robbed of its wonder. But it flutters down, soundlessly, hour after hour while we are asleep. Outside the closed curtains of the bedroom, a vast transformation scene is taking place, just as if a myriad elves and brownies were at work, and we turn and yawn and stretch and know nothing about it. And then, what an extraordinary change it is ! It is as if the house you are in had been dropped down in another continent. Even the inside, which has not been touched, seems different, every room appearing smaller and cosier, just as if some power were trying to turn it into a woodcutter's hut or a snug log-cabin. Outside, where the garden was yesterday, there is now a white and glistening level, and the village beyond is no longer your own familiar cluster of roofs but a village in an old German fairy-tale. You would not be surprised to learn that all the people there, the spectacled postmistress, the cobbler, the retired schoolmaster, and the rest, had suffered a change too and had become queer elvish beings, purveyors of invisible caps and magic shoes. You yourselves do not feel quite the same people you were yesterday. How could you when so much has been changed? There is a curious stir, a little shiver of excitement, troubling the house, not unlike the feeling there is abroad when a journey has to be made. The children, of course, are all excitement, but even the adults hang about and talk to one another longer than usual before settling down to the day's work. Nobody can resist the windows. It is like being on board ship.

When I got up this morning the world was a chilled hollow of dead white and faint blues. The light that came through the windows was very queer, and it contrived to make the familiar business of splashing and shaving and brushing and dressing very queer too. Then the sun came out, and by the time I had sat down to breakfast it was shining bravely and

First Snow

flushing the snow with delicate pinks. The dining-room window had been transformed into a lovely Japanese print. The little plum-tree outside, with the faintly flushed snow lining its boughs and artfully disposed along its trunk, stood in full sunlight. An hour or two later everything was a cold glitter of white and blue. The world had completely changed again. The little Japanese prints had all vanished. I looked out of my study window, over the garden, the meadow, to the low hills beyond, and the ground was one long glare, the sky was steely, and all the trees so many black and sinister shapes. There was indeed something curiously sinister about the whole prospect. It was as if our kindly country-side, close to the very heart of England had been turned into a cruel steppe. At any moment, it seemed, a body of horsemen might be seen breaking out from the black copse, so many instruments of tyranny, and shots might be heard and some distant patch of snow be reddened. It was that kind of landscape.

Now it has changed again. The glare has gone and no touch of the sinister remains. But the snow is falling heavily, in great soft flakes, so that you can hardly see across the shallow valley, and the roofs are thick and the trees all bending, and the weathercock of the village church, still to be seen through the grey loaded air, has become some creature out of Hans

Andersen. From my study, which is apart from the house and faces it, I can see the children flattening their noses against the nursery window, and there is running through my head a jangle of rhyme I used to repeat when I was a child and flattened my nose against the cold window to watch the falling snow :

> Snow, snow faster :
> White alabaster !
> Killing geese in Scotland,
> Sending feathers here !

This, I fancy, must have been a north-country charm (for that grey upland region is full of wizardries) to bring down the snow. And though we are told by the experts that as much snow falls now as ever it did, we know better, and I suspect that the reason is that there are fewer children with their faces pressed against their nursery windows, chanting : ' Snow, snow faster ! '

This morning, when I first caught sight of the unfamiliar whitened world, I could not help wishing that we had snow oftener, that English winters were more wintry. How delightful it would be, I thought, to have months of clean snow and a landscape sparkling with frost instead of innumerable grey featureless days of rain and raw winds. I began to envy my friends in such places as the Eastern States of America and Canada, who can count upon a solid winter

First Snow

every year and know that the snow will arrive
by a certain date and will remain, without
degenerating into black slush, until Spring is
close at hand. To have snow and frost and
yet a clear sunny sky and air as crisp as a
biscuit—this seemed to me happiness indeed.
And then I saw that it would never do for us.
We should be sick of it in a week. After the
first day, the magic would be gone and there
would be nothing left but the unchanging glare
of the day and the bitter cruel nights. It is
not the snow itself, the sight of the blanketed
world, that is so enchanting, but the first coming
of the snow, the sudden and silent change.
Out of the relations, for ever shifting and
unanticipated, of wind and water comes a
magical event. Who would change this state
of things for a steadily recurring round, an
earth governed by the calendar ? It has been
well said that while other countries have a
climate, we alone in England have weather.
There is nothing duller than climate, which can
be converted into a topic only by scientists and
hypochondriacs. But weather is our earth's
Cleopatra, and it is not to be wondered at that
we, who must share her gigantic moods, should
be for ever talking about her. Once we were
settled in America, Siberia, Australia, where
there is nothing but a steady pact between
climate and the calendar, we should regret her
very naughtinesses, her wilful pranks, her gusts

of rage and sudden tears. Waking in a morning would no longer be an adventure. Our weather may be fickle but it is no more fickle than we are, and only matches our inconstancy with her changes. Sun, wind, snow, rain, how welcome they are at first and how soon we grow weary of them ! If this snow lasts a week, I shall be heartily sick of it and glad to speed its going. But its coming has been an event. To-day has had a quality, an atmosphere, quite different from that of yesterday, and I have moved through it feeling a slightly different person, as if I were staying with new friends or had suddenly arrived in Norway. A man might easily spend five hundred pounds trying to break the crust of indifference in his mind, and yet feel less than I did this morning. Thus there is something to be said for leading the life of a Jane Austen character.

THE NEW DIARY

THIS morning I suddenly remembered that I had not changed diaries, so I set to work and copied all the names and addresses and telephone numbers from last year's diary to this year's, a shiny green affair that is still regarded as an intruder by all the other inhabitants of my pockets. I am not yet accustomed to it myself, and regret that fat little blue one that was 1927 and that I threw into the fire when I had finished my copying. What I want with all these daft names and addresses and telephone numbers, I cannot imagine. They are not those of my friends, whose addresses and telephone numbers I always remember. Many of them belong to people I have not seen for years; they may have changed their addresses and telephone numbers and even their names by this time, for all I know to the contrary; and I do not care tuppence if they have or if I never see any of them again. Yet I go on copying these details from diary to diary, bridging the years with this superfluous scribbling, these mythical friendships. The fact is, I suppose, that I feel I must fill up some of these blank pages in the new diary. When I

53

open one of these things for the first time, I can almost catch the makers sneering at me somewhere in the background. ' What do *you* want with a diary ? ' I seem to hear them cry. And certainly I cannot possibly live up to one.

Thus, my new diary is clearly meant for a more important person. It has whole blank chapters, as it were, outside the range of my life. What, for example, is one to do with the dozen or so pages allotted to *Memoranda* ? Or with those headed *Letter Register*, and divided into three columns : *Name ; Received ; Answered* ? Are there people, outside banks and offices, who solemnly put down the letters they receive and the dates of their answers ? Then there are the *Cash Accounts*, from January to December ; the *Annual Cash Summary* ; and—not least, I trust—the *Cash Account— Special*. To grapple at all with these columns is to turn oneself into an accountant. Following Dr. Johnson, I hold it foolish for a man to account to himself how he has spent his own money, and the thought of these columns waiting expectantly in my waistcoat pocket would ruin all my pleasure in spending. I should walk abroad like a moving joint-stock company, and begin to see all life as so much double-entry, the world a ledger. There is nothing that takes away all zest for living as this fearful and secret accountancy. That is why those little lists, ' How a Man May Live

The New Diary

on Two Pounds a Week', are so curiously depressing. It is not the poverty they reveal —for most of us have made shift on such sums— but the way in which every penny is portioned out and accounted for, that is so depressing. Even out of two pounds, there should be some residue, half a crown or five shillings, left for sweet carelessness, eluding the sharpest cashier, gone down the wind of pleasure. I cannot understand the persons who fill in these columns. But perhaps there are no such persons.

Then last of all, my diary offers me pages headed *Notes for* 1929. If, by the end of this year, there are any inscriptions on these pages, I will wager that they will run 2 *lbs. butter— white stuff same as before* 4 *yds.—tobacco—hair- cut—try Bank?* and will have nothing whatever to do with 1929. Thus there is nearly one-half of my diary, what with memoranda, letter registers, cash accounts, and notes for the next year, outside the range of my life. And that, I fancy, is why I try to grapple with the *Addresses* section, and find myself copying lists of names and addresses I do not want from diary to diary about this time every year. If I lose this little green book—and it is for ever falling out of my pocket—the finder may sneer at me for having no memoranda, no letters to register, no cash to tabulate, and apparently no plans for 1929, but he cannot say, on the evidence before him, that I have no friends.

Apes and Angels

This is the time of year when I feel that I have plenty of friends—though their names and addresses cannot be found in my diary—and see myself as a brisk and sociable being. Glancing through my old diary this morning, I could not help noticing how brisk and sociable and vaguely important I seemed to be during the early months of last year, for the pages covering that period were quite respectably dotted with engagements: 'Lunch with So-and-So'; 'Tea at the Such-and-suches'; 'Dinner with What's His Name'. I saw myself happily trotting round from one to the other—that self of a year ago—an odd but not unenviable creature. Then the entries seemed to fade out until at last the pages passed in virgin sequence. Had I been dropped by every-body? Had I turned hermit? Not quite, I re-membered, but I had gone to live in the country or—as one paragraphist put it—I was then 'living in seclusion'. I like the paragraphists, even though they do spend most of their time apparently admiring bad authors. I like the way they write. Some people, innocent out-siders who do not understand these matters, think these gossip paragraphs are very clumsily put together. But when you consider that these gentlemen are engaged in a kind of alchemy, turning very vague gossip about people they do not know into what appear to be secrets from a midnight conference with

The New Diary

those people, you will agree with me that they contrive most artfully.

The sight of these blank engagement pages in my diary raises in my mind, like some grisly phantom, the problem of social life. Of all the dilemmas that a proud, foolish, sensitive, idiotic creature is faced with, this of social life is, to me, one of the most baffling, annoying, saddening. It can be simply stated : if I am not seeing many people, I wish I were ; if I am seeing them, I wish I were not. Give me a full diary, a week's round of engagements, and I look at my little book and take out my dress clothes and polish up my brightest impromptus, brisk and happy and convinced that the social fabric, now shimmering before me, drapes the world most radiantly. But long before I have worked through those engagements, I am tired of it all. I begin to pine for solitude. I find myself falling into Carlylean moods ; I tell myself, as I look round at the smiling faces and hear the chatter, that it shall not avail them ; I wonder at myself for ever consenting to appear, and vow that it has happened for the last time ; I recollect that no great things are done among such ' vain, deluding Joys, The brood of Folly without father bred ' ; I ask for nothing but long hours of work, meditation, loitering in remote places, the simplest pleasures of a distant home. By the end of the week, the mows and grins, the

5

unceasing talk about nothing, the tinsel and spangles of these relations with fellow-creatures, leave me irritated or depressed, and I close the door with relief and feel that at last the real world, offering the solid sustenance of lonely weeks only broken by a genuine friend or two, stretches before me.

The little book is shut up with a snap, and no more entries find their way there, except those concerned with tobacco and hair-cuts and visits to the bank. I am my own man again. Now for *Il Penseroso*! Now for solitude and the great work! 'What's become of him?' I hear them saying: 'Why does he never come near us?' If I could actually hear them saying this and could then quietly creep away, all would be well. But I only hear it in imagination, and then only for a few days. Very soon I begin to have a disturbing feeling that I am not being missed, that my acquaintances are all so busy enjoying themselves— mere foolish gadding about, of course, a shocking waste of time—that they have nearly forgotten my existence. However, having discovered a better way of life, that is nothing to me, and I spend a day or two pointing out to myself what a better way of life it is. And then, for some sickening reason, nothing happens at all. Nobody comes to see me. Nobody invites me anywhere. It does not matter, of course, because—as I tell myself time after time—I am

The New Diary

only too jolly glad to be out of it all. But then I begin to feel *really* out of it all, and this is quite a different feeling, much less pleasant. Apparently nobody cares a rap about me. Apparently it does not matter how decent you are to people, how much they may pretend to like you, they forget all about you in a week or two. Then I am visited by a shining and tantalizing vision of *L'Allégro* ; I see and hear from afar the smiling faces and the friendly hum of voices ; and all resistance vanishes. How sick I am of lumping about alone ! What a lout I am becoming ! And then at last— happy moment !—the invitations arrive again and the little book pops in and out of my pocket, and all is well. So begins the round again, and all is not well. What can we do, my diary and I ? There is, I shall be told, some happy mean, some nice adjustment of solitude and company, that will release us at last from this circle of sad enchantment. I have no doubt there is, but I have not found it, and meanwhile the little books come and go with hastening speed, like the leaves and the flowers, the summers that were once an age and are now only a hurried magic of blue and green and gold.

THE WICKED PEOPLE

I WAS very sorry to learn the other day, from an article in a newspaper, that Hollywood has now reformed itself. It appears that at one time (as we all imagined) these strange beings of the film world, whose lucky shadows are so familiar, did indulge in nights of furious pleasure and fling away recklessly the fortunes their shadows brought them. But now, we are told, they have made an end of the old bad, mad ways ; they improve their minds and creep to bed at ten o'clock ; they invest their surplus cash in the tinned fruit trade ; they cultivate the domestic affections and, over the grape fruit and cereals, look at the same wife or husband month after month. Apparently some pressure has been put upon the wilder spirits, and ' morality clauses ' have now been inserted in all contracts. It is evident that the film magnates believe that the public does not like to spend its evenings watching the pictured antics of improper persons. This may be true of the public in America, which would seem to have a character of its own. I have never been to the United States and I do not profess to understand them. Every American newspaper

The Wicked People

I have ever read has given me a glimpse of a world so fantastic that I find it difficult to believe in its real existence. But what may be true of the American public is not necessarily true of the people of this older and more sophisticated and sadder continent of ours. For our part, we do not want very proper film actors and actresses and a reformed Hollywood. We like to imagine them as very reckless and dissipated creatures defying the conventions, outraging the dull respectabilities. We like to think of Hollywood as a glorious sink of iniquity, full of drink and dope and illicit love, scarlet nights and unrepentant mornings, fortunes flung away to gratify a whim.

This drab transformation is very disheartening. We do not know where to look now for our wild fellows, mad bad girls, haunts of luxury and vice. And—this is the point—we must look somewhere. We may not exactly want to live that kind of life ourselves but we do want somebody to be living it somewhere. We must have one set of people and some place to regard with mingled envy and disapproval. There must be some devil-may-care images, some wicked and highly coloured stuff, with which our imaginations can play. We may have banished this splendid wickedness— swaggering past in velvet on its way to the Devil—from our own lives, but that does not mean that we desire to banish it from the world.

Apes and Angels

It is essential that it should be going on somewhere, so that young people can dream and
know rich envy, old people be warmed by the
pleasant heat of disapproval, our wild lads
have a goal and our preachers a red-hot text.
So far the world has contrived that its honest
folk shall not be disappointed, and has always
been able to offer them some place where life
was all gilded and vicious and crazy, has shown
them some set of wicked people, roaring blades
and lovely doxies.

Who have always been the most popular
kings ? The rakes and the rips, whose courts
have been notorious for their profligacy, who
have emptied the public purse debauching
themselves and their wild followers. Charles
does nothing but sup with his mistresses, laugh
with his rakehell wits, and quietly sell the
country, but he keeps his crown through bad
times and good and always has his ' God save
you ! ' as he rolls through the streets. His
sour brother James takes his place, turns pious,
and is next found creeping out of the country.
George the Third lives the life of a Presbyterian
elder and is more unpopular than his grand-
father ; but his son, Regent and fourth George,
an ass but one of the dandies of the town, is
everywhere huzzahed. Who are the rulers who
have lost both crowns and lives ? Timid
respectable stay-at-home citizens like Louis the
Sixteenth and the late Tsar, men who really

The Wicked People

ought to have been keeping small grocer's shops. We are told that rebellion and revolution arrive when at last the licence of aristocracy passes all bounds. This is nonsense. It is when the aristocrats are no longer the dashing wicked people, swaggering down into hell-fire, that the crowd decides it will have no more of them. The crowd wants something for its money, a day-dream, a bad example, a text, and refuses to support a number of persons who stay at home at night, live plainly, and dabble a little in science. The tumbrils have always been filled, not with the notoriously depraved creatures, but with dull aristocrats who have taken to imitating the virtues of the middle classes. If there are to be gentry, with special privileges and pockets gaping for money, then there must be ' goings-on '. A revolution is a substitute for ' goings-on ', the absence of which leaves a painful blank in the popular imagination.

At one time poets and artists were included among the wicked people. It was said that they threw their money away, drank like fishes, stopped up all night and stayed in bed all day, made love all over the place. The result was that some people condemned them, many others envied them, and the remainder, the wisest, regarded them with interest, enjoyed their life at second-hand as a kind of moral holiday. Meanwhile, poetry and art flourished. They borrowed glamour from the lives of the wicked people who produced them. Even the godly were fascinated, crept up to sniff the brimstone. But now the poets and artists have lost their old reputation, and everybody knows that they are quite respectable, that their company might even be improving for one's wife and children—and what is the result ? Why, nobody cares tuppence now for poetry and art. It is the same with the Stage. Actors never made a greater mistake than when they rid themselves of that old fascinating air of vagabondage and became plain citizens, with an account at the local bank, visiting cards, and an ordinary domestic life. Those were the great days of the Theatre when the actors and actresses were still considered the wicked people. ' On the stage ' meant something then : there was a thrill in the phrase. Playgoers could whisper to another the last tit-bit of news that had somehow escaped from behind the scenes, where there were supposed to be endless ' goings-on '. The leading gentleman was drinking himself to death, and the private life of the leading lady was one huge crimson scandal ; everybody was very shocked and did a little head-wagging, but everybody was thrilled too and was ready to walk miles to see one of these reckless creatures.

Kings and Courts, aristocrats and the great houses, poets and artists and the Latin Quarter,

The Wicked People

actors and behind the scenes, all these persons
and places have gradually exiled themselves
from the popular imagination, which at last did
not know where to turn to look for a new set
of wicked people, a new seat of luxury and
vice. Something was attempted with the
millionaires, particularly in New York, but
they never held the imagination. Probably
Carnegie and Rockfeller were always in the
way. Then came the films and Hollywood,
and at last the situation was saved. Once
more the world had its wicked people, its sink
of iniquity, and everybody was happy and the
American film industry flourished. The sinister
rumours spread, the legend grew, and more and
more picture palaces had to be built. And
now Hollywood has been reformed. Here is
the great opportunity of the British film
people. I notice that a new organization, on a
very large scale, called ' British Incorporation
Pictures ', has been formed to challenge the
huge American concerns. What this organization, with its fellow British companies, should
do is to take over some rather out-of-the-way
town, such as Kendal or Truro, fill it with
studios and hotels and cabarets, and give out
that it is now the most vicious place in the
world. No pains must be spared to swell and
spread the legend of wickedness. It must be
pointed out that while American film players
are sitting quietly at home, knitting and studying

tinned fruit returns, the British players are all recklessly spending their youth and beauty and large fortunes in gaming, drinking, doping, fornication, that few of them can last much longer, and that they are without a doubt the world's most wicked people. That will be quite enough : the British film (even though it still remains the feeble, tepid, botched thing we all know) will suddenly leap into world-wide popularity. Whole populations will shake their heads over newspaper articles disclosing, fully for the first time, the infamy of Kendal (or Truro or whatever the town is), the dreadful ' goings-on ' behind the British screen ; and whole populations will crowd in to see the very next British film. I suggest that a beginning should be made by the insertion of ' immorality clauses ' in contracts.

THE DARK HOURS

THIS last week I have had a succession of bad nights. It is not merely that I cannot easily find sleep. This I never could do, except during those times when I have spent the whole day in the open. Who, having enjoyed them, does not remember those hours of sleep, a divine unconsciousness, that fell on him, came down like a vast benevolent sandbag on the top of his head, at the Front ? Sleep then was not simply a dark little ante-room through which one passed in order to arrive at the next morning's breakfast table, but a sojourn in the Blessed Isles. I remember—it must be twelve years ago—the best sleep I ever had. We had been three weeks or so in the trenches, the clayey kind, full of water and with hardly a dug-out ; and though there had been no real fighting, there had been any number of those daft alarms and excursions that hearty generals, talking over the wine and cigars in some distant château, praised to one another, in the belief that Englishmen always preferred magnificence to war. We had been so long without adequate sleep that our eyes were for ever hot and staring under leaden lids. Well, one dark night we were relieved at last, and went swaying down miles of cobbled road. Some of the fellows dropped out, others slept as they staggered on, and finally a remnant of us arrived at some place that was nothing to us but a dark assemblage of barns and windowless houses, familiar enough yet as unreal as a place on the moon. A gulp or two of hot sweet tea, a moment's glow of rum, then down we fell so mud-caked that we were as stiff as mummies on the hard floors, and down too came the lovely velvet curtain, blotting out the whole lunatic show of babbling statesmen and lads with glazing eyes. I slept for eighteen hours.

In the ordinary way, however, I have to woo my sleep, and that is one reason why I have read so many books, chasing Morpheus down innumerable labyrinths of eighteenth-century moralizing or twentieth-century introspection. Those no‑sooner‑have‑I‑touched‑the‑pillow people are past my comprehension. There is something suspiciously bovine about them. When they begin to yawn about half-past ten, as they always do when I am with them (and I make you a present of the inevitable comment), I feel that they forfeit all right to be considered as fellow-creatures, spirits here for a season that they may exchange confidences at the hour when all the beasts that perish are fast asleep. I do not complain about having to approach sleep so stealthily, tip-toeing through a chapter

The Dark Hours

or so. After all, this is only to prolong the day, and I cannot help thinking that such a reluctance to part for ever from the day, though it be only an unconscious reluctance, is proof of an affectionate nature, unwilling to dismiss a servant, however poor a thing. Nor do I complain—though I like it less—about waking too early, beginning the day before it is fairly ready for me, nothing but a grey little monster with the chill on it and still opposed to all our nobler activities. I have been told that as the years wither me away, I shall have more and more of these early wakings, and I cannot say that the prospect pleases me. But for the moment I will submit to it without complaint, for there are worse things, and all this last week I have been suffering from them. I have been finding myself awake, not at the end of one day nor at the beginning of another, but sometime between them, in the mysterious dark hours.

Now this I do most bitterly resent. I have accustomed myself to prolonging the day, and I will try hard to resign myself to beginning it before it is worth beginning, but this other thing, this awful interloping piece of time, neither honest to-day nor splendid to-morrow, is a horror. You suddenly wake up, open your eyes, expecting welcome daylight and the morning's post and the savour of breakfast, only to discover that it is still dark, that nothing is happening. You roll over, turn back, then over again, curl your legs up, stretch them out, push your hands under the pillow, then take them out, all to no purpose : sleep will not come. You have been thrust, a dreadfully alert consciousness, into some black No Man's Land of time. Reading, for once, fails as a resource. Frequently your eyes are so tired that the lines of print become blurred and run into one another. But even if you have no difficulty in seeing, it is still hard to read because all the savour seems to have departed from literature. You feel as if you were trying to attack a dish of cold potatoes. Even a new play by Shakespeare would leave you indifferent. I remember spending one very hot night in a London hotel. The place was full and I was a late-comer, so that I was given a tiny bedroom not far from the roof and looking out on nothing but a deep narrow court. I got off to sleep very quickly, but awoke about two and then vainly tossed and turned. There was nothing for it but to read, and I switched on my light. As a rule I have a book in my bag, but this night I was completely bookless, and the only reading matter in the room was that supplied by two evening papers. I had already glanced through these papers, but now I had to settle down to read them as I have never read evening papers before or since. Every scrap of print, sports gossip, society chit-chat,

The Dark Hours

City Notes, small advertisements, was steadily devoured. There I was, in my hot little aerie, reading those silly paragraphs about Lord A leaving town or Miss B the musical comedy star making puddings, while the night burned slowly away. For weeks afterwards the sight of an evening paper made me feel depressed.

Yet it is even worse when your eyes refuse to help you and even the silliest reading is impossible. You are left with your thoughts, as I have been several nights this last week. It is not possible, I find, on these occasions to think constructively or amusingly at all. You cannot plan anything. You cannot even lose yourself in an entertaining reverie. The dark hour, belonging to no day, swoops down and claims you as its own. No longer do you float easily on the kindly tide of ordinary human affairs. There is nothing tangible that you are afraid of, and, indeed, a burglar or a little outbreak of fire would seem a blessing. Nor are you, in melodramatic fashion, the prey now of your conscience. But you are alone, completely alone, really feeling for once that you are imprisoned in your consciousness. At ordinary times we seem able to reach out of ourselves, sometimes entirely forgetting ourselves ; and that way lies happiness. In these dark hours there is no escape, not even by any dizzy ladder of thought, and your mind goes round and round, drearily pacing its cage. Life

is nothing but a pulse beating in the darkness,
or, if not that, then only the remembrance of
a vague happy dream, bright faces fading and
suddenly dwindling laughter, surrounded and
conquered by terrible night. But this is only
life, as it were, outside yourself. Inside you, there
is life too, something alive, sensitive, shuddering,
a bird beating its wings against the bars.

This self-consciousness of the dark hours,
unable to fasten on anything outside itself, for
ever denied communication, its thoughts wearily
jangling round the old circus ring of the mind,
is a glimpse of Hell. These are the terrors
with which the preachers should threaten us.
The old-fashioned place, we know, would soon
become companionable. I have no doubt that
it would not take us long to develop a taste
for molten metal and brimstone, and that the
fiends themselves would soon prove to be most
entertaining companions. But these dark hours
of the night and the spinning mind, if prolonged,
would only gain in terror and despair. They
are the true nightmare. The very thought that
even now they are probably lying in wait for
me is infinitely depressing. And, for the time
being, I am avoiding a certain kind of fiction,
if only because it has a curious suggestion of
this torment. The kind I mean consists of
quite clever stuff by youngish contemporary
novelists, who work entirely and very elabor-
ately through the mind of one central figure,

The Dark Hours

whose self-consciousness, inability to escape
from self, are so extreme that he or she is really
a solipsist. Never once do these unhappy
creatures forget themselves. They are for ever
watching themselves, and relating everybody
and everything to that image. And always
they are depressed and depressing. In theory
these novels would seem to grapple very closely
with life, but somehow in practice, as actual
representations, they fail badly, as everybody
who still clings to the unfashionable practice of
comparing literature and life must recognize.
I realize now, however, that they do represent
something with tolerable accuracy, and that is
the night's vengeance on the unsleeping consciousness, the dark hours.

where sailors determined that they, in secret, learn and without some shadow that is really a shadow. Men once do those unhappy creatures reveal themselves. They are for ever watching, therefore, and finding everything, and everything in that shadow. And I hear

HATS

FOR the last twelve months I have been told that I ought to get a new one, and now I suppose the time has come. The one I have now is still what I should call serviceable, but if I were pressed—and lately the pressure has been constant—I should be compelled to admit that it has neither shape nor colour. It has been through innumerable downpours, has spent hours on luggage racks squashed under other people's suit-cases, has been kicked about under miles of theatre seats, and time after time has been lost and found. I have known the day when it was stiff with ice and I have also known the day when it shaded my head from the tropical sun. It is a hat that has served me nobly, and if only I were allowed to look for another one exactly like it, all would be well. But the order has gone forth that I must get a new hat that will be quite unlike the old one ; I must get a ' decent hat '. Now the problem is, where am I going to find this decent hat ? I cannot wear a cap because—I am told—it makes me look like a ruffian, or, to be more exact, like a member of one of the more disreputable race-gangs. A bowler is

Hats

unthinkable : it would turn me into a comedian, and a comedian with an aching head. The straw hat appears to have vanished from the brows of men and it never was a hat for me. (I used to know a man who wore one all the year round. What's become of him ? What becomes of all the queer people we knew when we were young ?) Obviously, I cannot go about for ever wearing a topper, though the notion is by no means unattractive. The panama and the deerstalker are not my style, and the sun helmet, the turban, the Glengarry, and the fez would all demand more courage in the wearer than I can supply. There remains nothing but the common soft felt hat.

Well then, I hear you exclaim, there are plenty of them about : go and buy one ; or, as one or two of my friends, I regret to say, might put it : buy one and have Dunn with it. The trouble is, however, that I am a man not easily hatted. Indeed, so far as my head is concerned, the times are out of joint. In another age, when men wore flat velvet caps or three-cornered hats or chimney pots, I might have been able to walk into the nearest shop and discover what I wanted ; but in these days there is nothing that will be exactly right and the best I can hope for is a poor compromise. My present hat is a compromise and if I depart from it I must necessarily fall into absurdity, yet I am commanded not to buy another like

75

it. One does not even receive any help from the papers nowadays. What has become of all those grave and fastidious gentlemen who used to write on men's fashions, the Majors and Barons of yesterday? I can remember reading them and enjoying them even when I was a boy and did not care how I was dressed. I think I must have enjoyed the atmosphere they created. 'A black tie with small red spots,' they would tell us, ' is being worn with the lounge suit this season.' And then again: ' The lapel is smaller than ever and breast pockets are being introduced once more.' Ah! —the Majors and the Barons. Their world came crashing down; and we sit in its ruins crying, Where be your red spots and your lapels now?

There are, roughly, three kinds of felt hats: the common English hat, which has a narrow brim, the wide-brimmed Latin hat, and the wide-brimmed American one. Now the ordinary English one does not suit me at all. Its brim is so small that my face seems to bulge out underneath it, and I look like a man who is about to sing a comic song. I have tried on dozens of these hats (staring at myself in those sickeningly well-lighted mirrors that the hatters provide) and the only difficulty I have had has been in deciding which one was the most ridiculous. I have tried to obtain the requisite width of brim by taking the very largest hat

Hats

in the shop (I take a large size anyhow) and putting paper inside the leather band so that the hat would not slip down over my ears; but that would not work because the crown looked too big and the brim still looked too small. I have gone to the other extreme and bought hats with enormous brims, hats from the ends of the earth. These hats did not make me look absurd, they simply transformed me into another and very different kind of person. As soon as I clapped my hat on, I felt like a man at a masquerade, and as I walked about the streets peering out from under their verandas I wanted to explain to everybody I met that I was not the creature I seemed. My one desire is to escape notice, to have enough brim to pass me in the crowd, but as soon as I escape from the miserable inch or so of felt that our own hatters give us, I find that I have to turn myself into a wildly picturesque person. There was a brief season during which I walked about looking like the Sheriff of Rising Star, Texas, the rough fellow of the big open spaces with the heart of gold; and small boys nudged one another when I passed.

I have had an adventure with the enormous Latin hat. An artist I know once returned from Italy with the very largest black felt hat I have ever seen outside the theatre and the pictures. This colossal sombrero was a present for me. He insisted upon my wearing it and he assured me that I had found at last the perfect hat. For one week I wore it, made my plans and dreamed my day-dreams in its vast shade, but I knew from the first that my friend was wrong and that I was making a mistake. It was a hat for conspiracies in the little café just off the Plaza, for a grand passion among the orange-trees. It was a hat for non-representational art or expressionist drama, for a brand new theory of aesthetics, for the worship of the latest foreign fraud. It was a hat for an Aldous Huxley character, one of those descendants of *Le Neveu de Rameau*, and perhaps if I had worn it for about twelve months I should have begun to imitate these queer beings and should have passed my time between pessimistic philosophizing and cool and casual fornication. But it was not a hat for me. If I had worn a false beard, I could not have felt more uncomfortable. It was a relief to be hatless and to discover oneself again. How long I should have worn it, if the decision had been left with me, I cannot say ; not long, I imagine ; perhaps another week at the most. It chanced, however, that fate itself intervened. That hat came to a sudden, a most unexpected, a really fantastic end. It was blown into the Thames. I was making my way across London Bridge one Sunday morning, having a train to catch at the station across the river, and there happened to be a lively breeze blowing downstream. That enormous spread of light felt was a temptation to every passing wind, and I was always compelled to hold it down. But when I was about half-way across, I heard the sound of martial music behind me, and turned to see two companies of Territorials marching past. I was so interested that I forgot to keep hold of my hat ; there came a sharp little gust ; and the next moment I looked down and saw my hat, like a great blackbird, half tumbling and half sailing down to the water. A rescue was impossible. There were no passing boats and nobody even noticed that my hat had gone. I have often wondered what became of it, for it was stoutly made and would certainly float, and somebody probably fished it out of the water.

Perhaps at this very moment it is swaggering down the main street of Singapore or Para. Perhaps some waterman found it and gave it to his girl. I hope so, for that was one advantage of the enormous wide-brimmed hats : they looked so becoming on women. During my well-brimmed days, I never found a hostess under forty who could resist the temptation of trying on my hat, and my hat always made them look charming, that is, even more charming than they usually look. My present hat, the one that has given me such good service, is not one of the Latin or American monsters, neither is it one of the common English variety. It might have been made, you might say, either at the extreme eastern edge of the United States or at the extreme western point of Ireland. It is, like so many good things, a compromise. It does not make me look like an English comedian, nor like the Sheriff of Rising Star, Texas ; it hits a more or less happy mean, and merely makes me look like one of Pinkerton's men, the burly fellows who chew cigars in the background of so many scenes in the films. I do not mind this and consider that I am getting off lightly, but apparently some members of my family either do not understand my difficulties or are simply tired of me in the Pinkerton man part, for the fact remains that I am ordered to buy a new hat and it must be different from the present one. Who was it that first produced the simile ' as mad as a hatter ' ? I wonder if it was an ancestor of mine.

REMINISCENCES OF TRAVEL

I NEED a new passport and spent a part of this morning filling in the application form. How annoying it is to be compelled to give your destination! What happens if you fill in that space with some defiant flourish of the pen, or reply 'The Five Continents', or 'From Prester John's Kingdom up to Trebizond'? This morning I merely had to put in 'France and Italy', and that gave me no satisfaction. No sooner had I set down their names than I realized that I did not really want to go to France and Italy. A man might just as well stay at home as go to France and Italy. I doubt if I have the slightest desire to set eyes on them again. I remember having a sudden impulse to strike out 'France and Italy', and to insert in their place, in block capitals, the following destinations: Slavonia, Ruritania, Grünewald, Cravonia, Eppenwelzen, and Maritime Bohemia. I have spent some happy days and nights in these little countries, have not visited them for years now, certainly not since 1914, and should like nothing better than to renew my old acquaintance with them. They are, I believe, harder to find and, when found,

to enter, than they were, and Messrs. Thomas
Cook & Son will no longer issue through tickets
to any of them. They tell me that it may be
possible to re-book in Illyria, but even then
transport is doubtful once you have passed the
frontier. I know for certain that so far as
Grünewald and Cravonia are concerned, the
difficulties are immense, because there is no
railway and no motor-bus service even yet, and
it is still a question of taking a barouche over
the high pass. You can walk in, of course,
just as we used to do in the old days, but now
that walking is not to be thought of, it means
a barouche, for the old rule still stands, I am told,
and the sentries will pass no other conveyance.
And where, I ask you, are we to find a barouche?

If I cannot go to any of these places—and
alas! my passport form has been sent in, with
nothing more than a timid request for France
and Italy in it—I will at least try to recapture
my old memories of them. The trouble is,
though, that all these countries have somehow
come to be confused with one another in my
memory, so that I cannot distinguish between
Slavonia and Grünewald, cannot definitely allot
a reminiscence to Ruritania or Eppenwelzen,
and find it impossible to declare whether I am
thinking of Cravonia or Maritime Bohemia. It
matters little, however, because I suspect that
you who read and remember with me will find
yourselves in the same situation. These six

Reminiscences of Travel

territories, with several more unnamed, have all run into one another to make up one shining mass of reminiscence. There is no help for it, particularly as it so happens that I have not a single map here to provide me with a few names that might locate a scene, an incident. The geographical background is woefully vague, but the memories themselves, standing out in lost sunshine and starlight, are clear enough. The sights and sounds are there, wanting only words to capture them. But how befuddling, how treacherous, are words !

Do you remember—it is the first thing that leaps to mind—a typical bright spring morning in the little capital ? A regiment of cavalry, magnificent in green and silver, goes jangling down the great avenue of the Limes, perhaps with its band. I can hear that march of the Royal Hussars now, and see the instruments flashing in the sun. You saw these soldiers as you walked down the avenue from the Hotel Bristol, where you are staying (and very snug you are, in a room with a balcony, for three or four golden eagles a week), to the Café de Paris, which every one in the capital, even Count von Stumpf and the revolutionaries, visits at about eleven in the morning to drink coffee, eat little cakes, and smoke long cheroots. Droll little Something-heim, chief clerk to the Chancellor, comes trotting over as usual, and you have a word with him as he passes on his way to his favourite table in the corner, and he tries to look important, and only succeeds in looking fussy and comical. Poor little Something-heim! I wonder if he still trots over to the café. Then there is a stir at the tables outside, and they are standing up and raising hats. The Princess has just gone past, as lovely as ever, with her dark-browed cousin in attendance. He has returned, then, from his castle and great estate on the hills. To-night we shall see him pouring out libations of champagne (which, after all, is cheap enough here, four silver marks the bottle) to Venus, in the company of the pretty little French dancer, newly arrived at the theatre, for whom he has deserted the passionate and jealous Countess von Thingumbob. There will be trouble there. It is said that he wishes to marry the Princess, who refuses him time after time. There is some talk of her looking too often at a handsome young stranger, a foreigner. When she has passed, one or two of the revolutionaries whisper behind their hands, and a jeering laugh or two is heard. Undoubtedly your friend, Captain Fritz, with whom you are to spend the evening, is right when he declares that trouble is brewing in the little kingdom. There goes the old Chancellor himself, his face wrinkled with deep policies. Who is that with him? Ah!—the Chief of Police, scowling heavily as usual. So the morning wears on.

Reminiscences of Travel

How pleasant it was, too, to leave the town for the country, to climb above the pointed red roofs up the roads to the high hills, past the vineyards, the water-mills, up through the pine forests ! You could stay a night or two at the inn up there, at the junction of the forest roads, and listen to the foresters roaring in the kitchen, have a crack with the old innkeeper over one of his tall slender bottles of wine, tease his pretty daughter, all smiles and ribbons, and watch her blushes when you mentioned the name of the tall young forester who was always hanging about the door. Or you might chance to be a guest, as I have been more than once, at one of the fantastic old castles on the frontier heights, where there were any number of frowning Counts and jocular Barons and charming witty ladies, and scandal over the cards, and plotting and counter-plotting over the wine. Never shall I forget the night when we heard the troop of horsemen come clattering up the steep road and the Princess herself, pale but bright of eye, swept in to tell us that she had just escaped from the capital. What nights, what adventures, we had then !

It was equally good to return again to the capital, to find your omelet still golden, melting perfection at the Hôtel Bristol, to smell the morning coffee at the Café de Paris, to watch the sunlight in the lime-trees, to be clapped on the back by friend Fritz who, as he twirled his moustache (which spelt danger to the younger Maids of Honour at the palace he guarded), would give you all the news. And the news was always either very naughty or very romantic, none of that dull stuff which fills the newspapers of the greater powers. That very evening you would perhaps dine with him at the mess, listening idly to the chaff, the toasts, the Hussar songs ; or you might visit the theatre of which the capital was so proud, and rightly, too, for it was a delightful little gilded box of French wit and Austrian melody ; or if you were lucky you might be summoned to the palace itself, to attend a reception, a ball, a fête, or even—for there were no limits to the audacity of this Court—a masquerade. There you had the intellectual pleasure of seeing all the pieces of this royal game of chess assembled on the board and one subtle move after another made under your very nose. There were His Highness, gay as ever, the Princess, lovelier than ever, the crafty and watchful Chancellor, the dark-browed cousin obviously thickening the plot, the jealous Countess von Thingumbob whispering to the Chief of Police, and with them pawns innumerable, peering, chuckling, flirting, scowling. The great room is a blaze of candelabra and orders and diamonds. Outside in the purple and scented night, a great moon rises above the riot of Chinese lanterns in the grounds. His Highness's band is playing a waltz. It never plays anything but waltzes, this band, but you do not care, it plays them so divinely. I can hear it now, can feel myself being swept round and round by the last mad twirling of the strings. And now it has stopped, and suddenly everything, Princess, courtiers, sentries, candelabra, the palace, the town itself, and the very rising moon, has been huddled away. I wish I had boldly put down Ruritania, Slavonia, and the rest, on my passport form. That simple action might have set some kind of magic working, so that my passport might have been endorsed for these kingdoms, I might have gone to Cook's and discovered that one of the clerks there was really a fairy, I might have been given a through ticket or directions for finding a barouche, a barouche to take me over the frontiers of reality.

TOO MANY PEOPLE

I HAVE decided that I cannot enjoy London any longer, not even on a short visit. I think it was our experience at the Circus that decided me. As soon as we arrived in town the other day we bethought ourselves of the Circus at Olympia and made up our minds to go that very afternoon. It never occurred to us to book seats. Having lunched, we descended upon West Kensington like gods, our minds pleasantly humming with anticipation and full of circuses. For my own part, I was bent on seeing the hundred or so clowns it promised us. Professional clowns and clowning, the silly antics of serious people, are rare enough these days, and would be a refreshing change from the other and unprofessional kind of clowning one knows so well, the serious antics of silly people. We were in good time, and I saw us strolling in and dropping into comfortable seats, surrounded by the enthusiastic youngsters who would make up the larger part of the afternoon audience. But when we arrived at the place, there seemed to be a revolution in progress. Olympia was being stormed as if it were another Bastille. Streams of people were coming away and great throngs were still pressing forward. Uniformed attendants, with very hoarse voices and waxed moustaches, and looking like the ringmaster's poor relations, were bawling out the news that all tickets for the Circus that afternoon had been sold. Notwithstanding their passionate reiteration, people, thousands and thousands of them, were still besieging the ticket-offices, perhaps in the hope of booking seats for the following week. Clearly we had arrived several days too late, and, feeling foolish, as one always does in these circumstances, we withdrew into the bustling wilderness of West Kensington, clownless and disconsolate.

This experience, from which I did not recover throughout our short stay, confirmed a suspicion I have entertained for some time, and I suddenly saw why it is that I enjoy these visits to London less and less. There are too many people in the place. One does not, of course, expect the city to be empty (how horrible it would be if it were !) ; the hum and bustle, the stream of strange folks, are inseparable from one's thought of the town, and are indeed part of its attraction ; and I am not crying out here for vacant lengths of street, empty theatres, and deserted restaurants. I do not want a whole city to myself, even if, in my heart of hearts, I believe that I ought to be supplied with one if necessary. But there is a point past which a cheerful and comfortable bustle and busyness turn into detestable overcrowding, not heightening our pleasure but robbing us of it. We are elbowed out of enjoyment, so hustled and harassed in our search for entertainment that we had better be working. This is what seems to me to be happening in London. Not so many years ago there were just enough people about, in the streets and buses and shops and theatres and restaurants, to animate the scene, giving it movement and colour and dramatic interest, so that one felt one was seeking pleasure in the world's capital and enjoyed the gregarious thrill ; but at the same time there was ample room to move and enjoy at ease, and there was no necessity to push and jostle and book seats and rush for tables. Now it seems—it may be my fancy, for I have no figures to support me ; but there it is—that happy state of things has vanished, and as year follows year there seem to be more and more people walking the streets, waiting at shop counters, jumping on buses and tube trains, filling the theatres and hotels and restaurants and tea-shops.

Where they all come from, these people, I cannot imagine ; but there they are, and more and more of them. I find the very trains up to town uncomfortably crowded these days. At whatever hour of the day I venture into some streets, such as Oxford Street or Kensington High Street, I can hardly move along, so dense is the crowd. If I wish to go to a theatre, either

Too Many People

all the seats are booked for weeks ahead or there
is nothing left but some seat at the end of a back
row. Even in the afternoon the places are full.
My only chance of dropping into a comfortable
seat at a theatre at the last moment, it would
seem, will have to depend on my writing a play
myself and getting it produced. No matter
what hotel I stay at, there is hardly ever any
choice of rooms, and the lounge is always uncomfortably crowded from breakfast time to midnight. Lunch is a scramble for a table and a
disheartening tale of dishes that are ' off '.
There is not even a glimpse of solitude and quiet
at tea-time. Dinner is another adventure more
reminiscent of race-meetings and cup-ties than
the serene and noble hour of refreshment. A
late supper is not to be thought of, for by this
time one has not heart to push and jostle in the
chattering, gaping, elbowing mob. Even if,
suddenly sick of it all, I decide to rush away and
catch the very next train home, there is not a
taxi to be had to take me to the station. And
the trains that carry me back to the country are
still uncomfortably crowded. It is as if everybody had decided to leave the place the same
moment that I had, and yet when I return
again, they are all back, determined to crowd
into the same streets, to fill the theatre or
restaurant before I arrive, and equally determined not to miss anything, not to dine and
spend the evening at home, not to go to bed.

Apes and Angels

Where do they come from ? Who are they ?
Why do they not go and do some work, or visit
a sick friend, or take a holiday in the Sudan ?
Why is it that there are more and more of them
every time I visit the city ?

As soon as I am back in the country, the
newspapers inform me that everybody has left
town or that there is a ‘ slump ’, and that
theatrical managers and restaurateurs are com-
plaining, but there are never any signs of anybody having left or of these ‘ slumps ’ the next
time I arrive in town. And I have never been
a lover of crowds, and now find myself disliking
them more and more. If my pleasure depends
upon my pushing and jostling and snatching
and grabbing among a crowd, I would rather go
pleasureless. If I found Paradise itself crowded,
with long queues waiting for wings and harps,
I should ask to be turned out ; but they will
surely order things better up there, and will
reserve their crowding for the other region.
I could devise a very pretty Hell for myself.
It would be one long Oxford Street without
any side-roads whatever, and everybody would
be compelled to keep moving, except certain
fiends, assuming the shape of stout middle-aged
women, all umbrellas and elbows, who would
be for ever wheeling round and standing and
staring. All food and drink would have to be
procured at cheap tea-shops, gigantic establishments deplorably understaffed and steaming

Too Many People

with humanity. Enormous crowds would be pushing their way in and out of these horrors all day, and anybody who did not join them, pressing in, elbowing a way from floor to floor, standing about for a seat, then banging a bell for hours, would have to go without bite or sup. There would be no homes at all to go to, but just this endless crowded street, and at night the doomed soul, which would be attached, of course, to a weary carcass, would have to seek accommodation in an hotel. There would be thousands of these, huge, cheap, nasty places, and nine out of ten would always be full, so that the wretched creature would be compelled to trail from one to another, encountering the sneers and hollow laughter of demons in the form of reception clerks and night porters. The rooms, when secured at last, would always prove to be tiny garrets, and either distressingly hot or insufferably cold. In all the crowds there would never be a familiar face ; day-long the faces would go jumbling by, sickening masses of them, pale faces, pink faces, long faces, short faces, whiskered faces, smooth faces, faces with beaks, faces with snouts ; but never a familiar face, never a friendly glance, an answering smile. This, I flatter myself, would be a most ingenious and devilish touch. But here is another. It is obvious that after a few weeks of this, most men would be so crowd-sick that they would suddenly begin screaming their hate of the throng about them, and would hurl themselves in the thick of it, determined to kill or be killed, or preferably both. They would want to batter in some of these idiotic faces, have one glorious baresark moment, and then, the infuriated mob retaliating, find happy oblivion. But, of course, they would not be able to do this. Their screams of rage would attract no attention, and their blows would not be noticed by the passers-by, being nothing but a kind of shadow play. Nothing would stop the procession of faces, the pushing and the jostling, the swarming crowd. I fancy that the Hell of Too Many People would occupy a respectable place in the hierarchy of infernal regions.

HOUSES

I HAVE been wondering if most of those 217,000 new houses are like the ones that have been built just down the road. They are very ugly indeed, square little boxes that look as if they had been nailed on to the landscape, and so ugly that even time will never beautify them. As the years pass and sun and rain come to tint the walls and roofs and the creepers climb to the eaves, these houses will mellow a little but they will never be beautiful. Down here, of course, we cry out at their hideous aspect. Our own houses have great charm, for either they are old farm-houses or cottages adapted to our needs or they are mansions designed by artists, and so we take tea together on our trimmed lawns or under our old oak beams and are all very indignant or superior about the ugly little houses that stare at us as we go by, not unlike rather pugnacious poor relations who have been invited for once to a grand party. But there are other people here —people we do not ask to tea, of course—who are happy and excited about those houses. They sit up at night wondering if they can afford to live in one of them. For years now, you see, they have been living with the wife's father or the husband's brother, crowded into a couple of tiny rooms, perhaps, and it has all been very uncomfortable and there have been little quarrels and they have not been able to ask their friends when they would have liked to, and when the husband was down with 'flu or the wife was having another baby it was so bad that life hardly seemed worth living. And now they may be able to have a place of their own, a lovely place with a proper sink and a sort of bath in the kitchen, if it will only run to it. So they go and look over those new houses, seeing them as a kind of signpost pointing to a sunlit main road of life; while the rest of us, fortunate or cunning enough to have installed ourselves snugly and picturesquely, hurry past the ugly little brick boxes to ask the Vicar's wife or Major Brown if it really is not too bad and if something cannot be done about it.

Even a local builder, you will notice, can suddenly turn our minds into a battlefield, where a desire for beauty wars with our common human sympathy. A few more of these houses and this place will no longer charm the eye; a great many more of them and it will be hideous; but on the other hand a number of people will have the chance at last of living decently and in comfort. The thorough-going aesthete, who admits to caring for nothing but his own

Houses

exquisite sensations, would have the landscape unspoilt though the remaining cottages should be crammed with wretched fellow-creatures. The rest of us, not being made of such hard glittering stuff, cannot help feeling that people should come first, that their chunks of happiness or misery are more important than certain delicate satisfactions of our own ; and it seems to us that the other way of thinking is like refusing to save a man's life because he has a detestably ugly face. We should be content to make the whole country hideous if we knew for certain that by doing so we could also make all the people in it moderately happy. Yet we know too that if the country were thus absolutely shut off from beauty, in the long run nobody would be really happy, for some part of the good life would be lost for ever. Thus once more we find ourselves faced not with a problem but an apparently insoluble puzzle which traps the mind into circular paths. (There are so many of these that I for one have ceased to have any opinions at all of any importance ; and sometimes I feel that we shall be compelled to start thinking all over again, in a new way.) We are left crying out upon the age that bore us. O cursèd spite !

But let us return to the ugly new houses. Is it possible that there is compromise between leaving people without a roof of their own and ruining the landscape ? Is it necessary that

most of these houses should look so unpleasant ?
I leave the answer to the town-planners, the
architects and the builders. All I can say is
that I do not understand why there is such a
general passion now for building semi-detached
or detached little houses. Do people refuse to
live in any other kind ? If they do, then I
refuse to sentimentalize over them any longer.
Let them stay with their husband's father or
wife's brother. I am convinced that it is this
detachment that is responsible for a great deal
of the ugliness. This it is that peppers the
country-side with little brick boxes. Even
those more lordly suburbs that are filled with
detached villas, not necessarily ugly in themselves, always depress me, if only because they
have such a higgledy-piggledy appearance, no
order or dignity about them. Moreover, they
eat up miles of good country-side, of meadow
and heath and woodland, making the town go
straggling on and on in the dreariest fashion.
I like town and I like country, but I must
confess that I do not like this half-and-half
stuff, neither one nor the other, these hill-sides
crazily dotted with villas, each bearing a mean-
ingless name. What is wrong with little
terraces and crescents and the like ? They
must be easier to build, and they are certainly
better to look at. Most of us have lived in
one of them at some time or other and found
there was nothing wrong with houses built on

Houses

this plan. Indeed, I am told they have certain advantages, being easier to warm and so forth. I believe that the best small houses built since the war, the model dwellings, were devised on this plan, arranged in short terraces or round three sides of a square. That is how civilized people should live, and not be camped each in his own detached bit of ugliness. Does not this, then, suggest a possible compromise between overcrowding and a country-side peppered with brick boxes? I ask the question out of my ignorance, wistfully.

Here is another. How is it that we are not for ever talking about houses and housing? Is it because those of us who do so much of the talking about things happen to be fairly comfortably and conveniently housed ourselves? I am not going to say how large my own family is, nor how many rooms we use, but I will say that if the number of those rooms was halved, my life would soon be very different and so, I suspect, would my point of view. It means that I should never be able to escape from the other members of my family nor they from me, that there would be little or no chance for quiet thinking or even talking, that if I remained at home my temper would be always on edge, that after a time I should neither stay in myself nor ask other people in to see me. In the country, one might manage in a tiny cottage because a good deal of time would be spent in the open. But in a large town, life in a very small house, of three or four little rooms, would be horrible. Either every sense would have to be blunted or existence would be a misery. In the West Riding town that I used to live in—and there are hundreds like it in the industrial North and Midlands—there were districts locally known as 'back o' the mill', and in these districts there were rows and rows of what were called 'passage houses', erected on a plan that enabled the contractor to build four houses in the space usually occupied, in slightly more civilized regions, by two small houses. Thus each of these dwellings, back to back as they are, has only one door, and not as a rule more than three rooms, a living-room and two bedrooms. These houses have not been demolished, they are there still, all over the North and the Midlands, I fancy. The children who attend the Council schools, where they are taught to sing or even to read the poetry of Shelley, live in such houses. When they leave school, they continue to live in them. Only a few are able to escape.

One of the objects of primary education, I believe, is to refine its small pupils, to make them more sensitive. This seems rather a dirty trick when we consider that the children have to return to those houses. It is very difficult to go on reading the works of Shelley in a room that has to be shared with all the rest of the

Houses

family and its various and frequently noisy concerns. It is hard to live the sensitive life when you are never alone. I think if most of us lived in such places with a growing family, we should let many things go if we were women, and get out as soon as we could and look for beer if we were men. Certainly we should either cease being sensitive or become embittered. I suspect that the absence of two or three rooms, in which a young man or woman might sit quietly and read or dream, has gone to make many a revolutionary just as it has gone far to make many a sot. There are some learned gentlemen, who sit in quiet studies thirty feet long by fifteen broad and consider the discontents of the lower classes, I should like to take by the hand and lead into one of those three-roomed houses, bidding them share the place with a noisy family for a month. A month would do, I think. At the end of that time they would be no nearer settling any of their problems than they were before, but there would be some things that they would understand. 'And all man's energies seem very brave,' says Mr. Squire, in his beautiful poem on a house. Well, they might even come to that conclusion too.

STIERISM

IT is more than likely that Herr Georg Stier is dead, for it is many a year since he wrote his 'Little English Talks: *Ein Hilfsmittel zur Erlernung der englischen Umgangsprache*', the speckled little book I picked up, the other day, in the sixpenny box. Just as Carlyle's Professor Teufelsdröckh pretended that his great work was nothing more than a study of Clothes, their Origin and Influence, so too Herr Stier pretended to aim at nothing more pretentious than a little work for the benefit of German students of the English Language. I suspect that he was another Teufelsdröckh. Was he writing only '*fur die höheren Knaben und Mädchenschulen*', as he declares on his title-page ? Not a bit of it. Writing back there in the comfortable 1900, he had a vision of what was even then stirring in the womb of Time. He knew, this philosophical dreamer, that one day, when the boys and girls had left their high schools and had grown up to a saddened manhood and womanhood, his little book would be discovered and recognized for what it was, not so many English talks but the first happy sketch of a new attitude towards

Stierism

life and an antidote to many philosophical poisons. I only hope that he is alive yet and that he may be given a few more years, to see Stierism conquer and save the world. This is not the place to give a fully reasoned exposition of the new attitude. No doubt a host of large volumes will soon make their appearance. Meanwhile, having been so fortunate in my visit to the sixpenny box, I see that it is my duty to become, for one week, what literary historians, in their curiously silly fashion, call ' one of the heralds of the new movement '. I will make one little cry in the wilderness and then depart, leaving the rest of the work to my betters.

It is only just that Central Europe, which has exported so much pessimism of late, so many mournful philosophies and drearily fantastic arts, should have provided this antidote to its poison. That is how I see Stierism—as an antidote. It is a happy realism, illuminated by an almost naïve but altogether delightful wonder. It begins at the very beginning of things, bidding us accept the world, take hold of life, with a zest not unmixed with serenity. Not that it takes refuge in a foolish optimism, closing its eyes to the evils of existence. It faces the facts, even the worst of them, as we may observe in these typical passages : ' The THROAT : Many people suffer with their throats, especially schoolmasters, teachers, singers, etc. These persons often **HAVE A SORE THROAT, FEEL AN IRRITATION IN THEIR THROAT,** they are **HOARSE, THEIR TONSILS ARE SWOLLEN,** so that **THEY HAVE A DIFFICULTY IN SWALLOWING.'** Again : ' The **BREAST** : When it is cold, when changes in the weather come too suddenly, we **CATCH A COLD, WE HAVE A COUGH,** a **NASTY** cough, **WE HAVE A GREAT DEAL OF PHLEGM ON OUR CHEST** and we have **TO COUGH** a great deal. Sometimes we also get **INFLAMMATION OF THE LUNGS.'** Or, better still, in this passage : ' The **STOMACH** : Happy the man who has a good stomach, which **DIGESTS** everything. Have you **A GOOD DIGESTION** or have you **A WEAK STOMACH** ? In order to escape the diseases of the stomach, we must eat proper food, we must indulge in no excesses, we must eat nothing between meals. Then we shall not be obliged to say : **MY STOMACH IS OUT OF ORDER, I HAVE STOMACH-ACHE, I HAVE A GASTRIC CATARRH, I HAVE A SPASM IN THE STOMACH (I HAVE INDIGESTION) ; THIS (or THAT) LIES HEAVY ON MY STOMACH.'** There is a good deal in this. To the authors of the last Expressionist drama or ultra-subjective and pessimistic novel, we might put some such pertinent queries : Have they a stomach which digests everything ? Does this (or that) lie heavy on their stomach ? The answer, if truthfully given, might explain some things that have seemed inexplicable.

Here and there, perhaps, Herr Stier takes too rosy a view of English things, but these are only slight slips and do not indicate any serious weakness in his attitude. Thus, his remark, in the section devoted to meals, that ' Each roast has its proper **GRAVY** ', shows a departure from strict realism. Possibly the subject brings out the old Teutonic strain of idealism in him. So, too, his statement, ' Our **HOUSEMAID** (our **SERVANT**) attends to our lamps every day ' should be accepted with caution. His picture of the tenant's life is also somewhat idealized : ' But now we are contented, for our flat is **ROOMY** and **COMFORTABLE** ; our **LAND-LORD** and **LANDLADY**, the **OWNERS** (the **PROPRIETORS**) of the house, are very nice, and our **RENT** is not too **HIGH**. And what are we to make of his account of boarding-houses ? He says : ' As in Germany, there are **BOARDING-HOUSES,** and they are the best thing for single persons who wish to learn English quickly, for here they always have plenty of opportunities to speak English.' This is hardly true, unless, as I suspect, the passage has a sinister meaning. Certainly there is satire in his paragraph on ties : ' Most gentlemen wear ties **WITH READY-MADE BOWS**. A tie **WITHOUT A BOW** is not for every one, for to make a bow, a good bow, is not so easy (requires a certain amount of skill). Many people wear **PINS** in their ties.' There is a fine irony in his account of **A FAMILIAR VISIT, A FAMILIAR CALL,** in which, after describing how he knocks, opens the door after being told to enter, apologizes for his intrusion, he shows us what passes then : ' " YOU ARE WELCOME ! WHAT ARE YOU DOING NOWADAYS ? IT IS AGES SINCE I SAW YOU LAST ! BUT SIT DOWN, PLEASE ! HOW IS IT THAT I NEVER GET A GLIMPSE OF YOU ? " " I HAVE BEEN VERY BUSY AND AM SO STILL ! " " INDEED ? " " WHAT ARE YOU DOING ? " So the conversation is begun and kept going.' That is an admirable thrust. So is his parting. 'UPON LEAVING and SHAK-ING HANDS, I say : " GOOD-BYE ! " Answers : " COME AND SEE ME AGAIN SOON ! GIVE MY COMPLIMENTS TO YOUR FATHER. MY KIND REGARDS TO YOUR MOTHER. REMEMBER ME TO YOUR BROTHER " (to your sister, etc.). I reply : " THANK YOU ! " ' And we too reply : ' Thank you ! '

But we have yet to come to Stierism proper, which is, I repeat, a happy realism, the facts lit with wonder. How it touches with wonder the commonest things, so that we discover a new joy even in dressing ourselves ! Turn anywhere in the section, one of the humblest, called ' Gentlemen's Toilet ', and its simple happy phrases create the world anew.

Stierism

' GLOVES. Gentlemen wear **GENTLEMEN'S GLOVES**; ladies wear **LADIES' GLOVES.**' Consider the matter of shoes : ' I have a good shoemaker. My boots always fit without **PINCHING (PAINING)** me. He makes use of good leather; the **UPPERS DON'T GET CRACKS**, the **SOLES (SINGLE** or **DOUBLE SOLES)** don't easily **TEAR**, so that I don't **WEAR OUT** many boots.' Herr Stier had his eye on us when he wrote this passage. He foresaw the time when any number of prominent persons would be always crying out because their boots pinched them. How few of our typical intellectuals could say that their uppers are uncracked and their soles untorn ! This passage is pure Teufelsdröckh. And then, for a return to a gay simplicity, an open-hearted acceptance of the world, consider the tiny paragraph on trousers, two short sentences that every pessimist should learn by heart and repeat as he dresses himself these grey mornings : ' **THE TROUSERS.** In summer, gentlemen wear **SUMMER-TROUSERS**; in winter, **WINTER-TROUSERS**. They are sometimes **WIDE**, sometimes **NARROW**, and are kept up by **(ELASTIC) BRACES.**' When such pessimists have mastered this, if they are given to writing criticism, they should turn to the walking-stick paragraph and meditate upon that for a season : ' A walking-stick is carried by many people ; it affords them some support in walking. The CANE (the SWITCH) serves only to give one countenance; the CUDGEL is not elegant and is out of the question.' Who does not know these Switch and Cudgel critics ?

There is nothing ascetic in Stierism. It believes in healthy and innocent recreation. In the chapter on 'The Town (London)', two quarters are specially noticed : 'The two most distinguished are the CITY and the WEST END ; the first is the BUSINESS quarter, the second the ARISTOCRATIC or HIGH LIFE quarter.' That 'High Life' is equal to a novel by Mr. Arlen. Our attention is drawn to 'The PUBLIC BARS, where you can have different sorts of beer'. A little farther on in the chapter there is a significant snatch of dialogue : 'Have you ever been present at a RACE-MEETING ? If not, go to one as soon as possible.' Stierism recognizes, too, that you may want to leave the town and high life. 'A man who is a GOOD WALKER, who does not easily TIRE, makes a walking tour from time to time. With a KNAPSACK on his back and a THICK STICK in his hand, he SETS OFF early in the morning.' Or he may ascend (climb) the mountain, spending the night, we are told, at a herdsman's cottage, and then climbing to the top next day. Then : 'After having rested, taken some refreshment and ENJOYED the beautiful PANORAMA which offers itself to his eyes, he goes down again,

Stierism

PLUCKING (GATHERING) RHODODEN-
DRONS and a BUNCH (or BOUQUET) OF
EDELWEISS, strengthened in both body and
mind.' We should like to see Mr. Arlen
returning to his high life from the mountain,
a bunch of rhododendrons in his hand. But
perhaps best of all, for it comes home shrewdly
to our bosoms, is a passage that is ostensibly
on the subject of wintry weather, but is really
a symbolical description, spiced with irony, of
this, our later day: 'At last IT THAWS,
the snow and the ice MELT (AWAY). IT IS
MUDDY. WHAT MUD! WHAT A QUAG-
MIRE! everybody cries. But they console
each other about it, for they know that this
bad weather will soon pass, that spring is
approaching, and with it, by and by, the fine
days.' I only wish they did.

AT THE CIRCUS

I DOUBT if I ever liked Paris so much as I did the other afternoon. We found ourselves near the Cirque d'Hiver and suddenly decided to see the matinée there. It was a most fortunate impulse, for we had unwittingly hit upon the one afternoon when the audience at the circus was even better than the entertainment, for it was *Mardi Gras*, and not only was the place filled with children, but it was largely filled with children in fancy-dress. The very ring itself could show nothing more colourful and fantastic and charming than the sight of the crowded tiers above, where the Lilliputian masqueraders chattered and laughed and pointed with tiny fat fingers. There were boxes—they might have newly come from a toyshop—crammed with miniature cowboys and washer-women and toreadors and pierrots and columbines. Just in front of us a diminutive Breton peasant woman and a little harlequin gasped and rocked at the antics of the clowns. On our right a three-foot soldier sucked away at a toffee stick, and our left-hand neighbour was a pocket nurse who bobbed up and down in ecstasy. This was clearly the ideal audience

At the Circus

for a circus. The crashing band in its high balcony, the shining and prancing horses, the ring-master and his brisk attendants, the acrobats who spent so much time turning in mid-air that they always seemed at once surprised and delighted whenever they found themselves standing erect, the clowns who always contrived to be rolled up in the big carpet and never really helped at all, they must have known that they had for once the audience of their dreams. I have seen more elaborate performances in the ring than that given at the Cirque d'Hiver, but I cannot imagine any circus that would please a child more or any adult who had not slouched too far away from childhood.

Surely it is the friendliest place of entertainment in the world ! Everybody there seems to know everybody else, and there are no barriers between performers and audience ; everybody is good-humoured and everything is open, friendly, accessible. During the interval we all wandered where we pleased. Many of the children, determined once for all to be circus performers or nothing, rushed down into the ring ; and its colossal mat, which obviously craved to be tumbled upon, was entirely at their disposal. So they ran and leap-frogged and somersaulted for a glorious twenty minutes, and the numbers of them, their fancy-dress, their happy antics, combined to make such a spectacle that it shamed the best attempts of the professionals, even the first grand entrance, the *Voltige Cheval et Charivari par les Clowns et Augustes*. The rest of us wandered round to the back, walking through the very entrances the clowns and acrobats had used. Here was no behind-the-scenes nonsense. You could go where you pleased, could pat the horses in their long stable opposite the buffet, could crowd round the open door of the dressing-room of the great Fratellinis and hear them talking to their friends, could jostle the ring-master and his assistants, and perhaps exchange a nod with the acrobat you had last seen flying in mid-air. All the performers seemed to be there, smoking cigarettes and pretending they were just ordinary mortals like the rest of us. I for one would not have been surprised if I had seen a couple of the Bengal Tigers enjoying a *bock* and a Maryland in the company of a juggler or two and a clown. What I did see was the happiest little boy in Paris. He was a minor member of a troupe of acrobats, who had just finished entertaining us by throwing one another about, but unlike the others this boy had not removed his ring clothes and make-up, and was leaning non-chalantly against the wall and surveying in a bored manner a crowd of boys his own age from the audience, all with envy written all over them. And I will wager that a company of the *Garde Républicaine* could not have kept that boy in his dressing-room during the interval.

We liked the horses and the tigers and the strong men and the Japanese jugglers, but the clowns we adored. How we laughed at the very serious one, dressed in a glittering court costume of clownage, who insisted upon turning the ring into a living-room and made all the assistants transform themselves into doors and windows and chairs and tables and even central heating apparatus ! But that was nothing compared with the shout that went up when the Fratellini, the three famous clowns of this circus, came on, waved to various friends in the audience, and then began making fun at furious rate. How delightful it must be to be a Fratellini ! It is true that one would have to paint one's face red and white, wear the most grotesque trousers and boots, and submit to being thumped and whacked and pelted with eggs. But consider the reward—the affectionate roar of welcome, the shouts of laughter, the delighted homage of a whole city, from unsophisticated little Jean Dubois to the very sophisticated M. Jean Cocteau. There was an advertisement on the circus programme that ran : ' *Restaurant " Aux Fratellini ", Le Rendezvous des 3 Célebres Clowns. Venez manger le plat préfere des Fratellini.*' Now that is real fame. That is to have arrived. What would some of us think if pages here suddenly blossomed with a similar advertisement. What a blushing there would be in Chelsea, in St. John's Wood, in Blooms-bury! But, alas!—both the giving and the receiving of such honours demand another temper than ours, and we must leave such things to the Latin races.

I must say that I enjoyed Les Fratellini as much as any infant present the other afternoon. I might not have been so shaken with laughter as the small boy just in front of me, the boy whose head was rolling helplessly over the edge of the box and who looked as if he were about to be sick at any moment; but that is not to say my enjoyment was less. Indeed, he was probably in pain, his small body being no longer able to survive with ease such strong gusts of laughter. I believe these famous clowns were not a success when they left their circus for the foreign variety stage, and this I can well believe. But in the ring of the Cirque d'Hiver they are completely at home, and offer the most robust and delectable fooling. How we laughed when the promised *boite de surprise* arrived and turned out to be a gigantic jack-in-the-box! How earnestly and yet fearfully did the white-faced one and the one who looked like an ancient dandy try to cope with the leaping monster! What a roar went up when they retired and the other one, that most grotesque and dilapidated figure with the fantastic nose and feet, came and fought with

the monster and finally took its place in the
box ! Then the other two returned and
brought with them an armoury of weapons,
long swords, air-guns, a cannon, and a pistol
as big as a dog-kennel. Immediately they
declared war on the box and its monster and
opened fire. They did not present any notes
or ultimatums or talk about the rights of the
nation or the needs of empire or the world
revolution. The monster in the box was
strange and so they determined to kill it. They
had a number of fine weapons and they wanted
to use them. And use them they did, until
they found at last it was not the monster but
their old comrade, the grotesque and dilapidated
one, who was inside, and then they burst into
tears and summoned a funeral party to come
and take away the box. But when the box
was raised, their comrade was left sitting on
the ground, and he was not dead after all but
was busy drinking out of a large bottle. He
was my favourite, the grotesque and dilapidated
one, for though he was so monstrously put
together that he hardly seemed a human being
at all, he was yet so filled with a wistful enthusiasm in his fantastic undertakings that he
seemed like a pathetic parody of the whole race
of men.

Just now, in Paris, that old flashing barometer
of Western civilization, there appears to be a
great enthusiasm for clowns and clowning.

Apes and Angels

Even the young intellectuals have taken them up. We have seen it ourselves in the widespread popularity of such people as Charlie Chaplin and Grock. The post-war world delights in its professional buffoons. As the interest in politics and some other things has declined, the interest in clowns has risen. I am certain that I care more now for such fooling as I saw the other afternoon than I would have done in the spring of 1914. Here is a problem for the philosopher. I wish Mr. George Santayana would give us one of his exquisite reveries on the subject. Why has the bruised and battered world suddenly become so fond of clowns? Is it because it is so bruised and battered and must now seek relief in easy laughter? That is an obvious explanation, but, of course, it will not do, for we do not want obvious explanations, which do nothing but make this life a trifle duller than it was before they were offered. Is it, then, because this clowning presents us with a shrewd parody of our life, hiding nothing, showing us plainly the vanity and greed and fear we display, how we whack and are whacked in turn? Is the sight of such buffoonery one of those escapes from life that suddenly turn into a sharp criticism of it? Do we laugh out of sheer relief, because it is all happening to some quaint creatures with white faces and red noses, and not, for once, happening to us, who sit for a

At the Circus

while and look on like the gods ? Is it worth
remembering that from the viewpoint of those
places in which the gods are supposed to rock
in inextinguishable laughter, the side of the
round world turned to them must look not
unlike a vast circus ring ?

SERVANTS

IN this matter, as in so many others, we have been unlucky in our generation. When our fathers set up house, there were servants to be had; and no doubt by the time my children grow up the domestic servant will be as useless as a horse. We have been born thirty years too late or too soon, just in time to see the maid make her final exit but too early to find a machine in her place. The house I live in at present is altogether charming, one of your rambling old small country houses or large cottages, the kind of house I always wanted my friends to have when I lived in London and for ever hoped to be packing a bag on Friday afternoon. I like the house, am even proud of it on certain fine Saturday mornings, when I see its reflection in the eyes of a visitor. The fact remains, however, that this house is about as well adapted to the conditions of to-day as a suit of armour. It demands the presence of three industrious, strong, cheerful, loyal female servants to conduct its affairs with anything like decency, and so far as I can see, it might just as hopefully demand the presence of three crossbowmen or alchemists. Thirty or forty

Servants

years ago, when there were still servants and the Registry Offices had not yet devoted themselves to idealistic fiction, I can well believe that this place was as snug as a Christmas Story by Dickens, as bright as a new toy, that all went with a swing ; but now that domestic service only finds a few recruits from the lower ranks of the unemployed, from the mere failures of the Labour Exchanges, this house is about as convenient a place of habitation as a Chinese junk would be among these Oxfordshire fields. It might be a vast pepper-pot, so many and violent are the sniffs we have heard. Indeed, for some time now it has not been a house at all, but a kind of annexe to the local Registry Offices, a waste-paper basket in which fabled cooks and languid house-parlour-maids deposit their more mendacious references.

Not at the moment, though. We have arrived at a crisis, for there is not a servant in the house. The work is being done by members of the household assisted by very temporary and spasmodic ' helps ', women from the village, who come in at odd times. Officially we are supposed to be in the last and worst straits, (' My dear, we're absolutely in despair ', you can hear us saying), but as a matter of strict fact we are more light-hearted than we have been for some months. There is now a happy picnic air about the place. We can go where we please, walk in and out of the kitchen quite unconcerned, and talk easily and loudly all over the house. Once more is dinner a jolly little meal and not a Dark Tower to our Roland. A cloud has been lifted from these old roofs, a weight of doubt and disappointment from our minds. No longer do we hear in the kitchen all our hopes go crashing with the ill-used crockery. Most important of all, ill-feeling, nay, downright hatred, has now left the house. It is terrible to live under the same roof with people who would appear to resent your very existence, to hate the very sight of you. These are hard words, and yet such has been our experience during these last few months. The servants we have had have not only been idle and inefficient, but have been from the first actuated by a most extraordinary resentment. Instead of being anxious and wistful house-holders, magnifying to one another every little scrap of decent service, we might have been tyrants who had just vetoed the constitution and doubled the taxes and the secret police.

It is all a mystery to me. If we had kid-napped these young women, if we had driven them to the kitchen range at the sword's point, they could hardly have been more resentful. Yet they came to us willingly enough—indeed, asked to come, nor were they deceived in any particular, for they were told what they were expected to do and how many miles we are from the nearest picture theatre, before they arrived. Why, then, did they all dislike us so much ? Was it our manner ? If so, these people must have a strong distaste for a timid, wistful, appealing, trying-to-make-the-best-of-you attitude. Perhaps they were disappointed when they dished up the first vile meal and discovered that we swallowed it without protest. Perhaps they were hoping I should start up, full of sound and fury, and fling plates across the hall, roaring great oaths and telling them to cook another dinner at once. Perhaps, admiring the pictures and sheik fiction, they wanted ' the rough stuff ', even in domestic service. Whatever it was, it was certainly no bullying on our part that aroused their resentment. You can imagine us hoping this time that all would be well, smiling at the new arrivals, gently hinting at what was to be done, loud in our approval when anything *was* done, and whispering to one another favourable verdicts. But even during the first few days they all began to glare hatred of us, and then when the dirt and the foully prepared meals were too much for our patience and we ventured a remonstrance they would toss their heads and fly into a rage. Then they would settle down into sheer hatred ; you could feel waves of it flowing out of the kitchen. A smiling idleness, like a dour efficiency, can be endured, but a scornful and scowling laziness and inefficiency are past the patience of men.

Apes and Angels

There is something sublimely impudent about this whole business of domestic service nowadays. Thus, a girl came to us as a cook, demanding the wages and privileges of a cook. Now this girl could not cook; she would not try to cook; she would not even try to learn how to cook; and at the least hint of criticism she either raged or sulked. It is just as if I agreed to write a certain number of essays, two thousand words long, for a paper, and the first week sent in about a thousand words not on any subject nor even making sentences, but merely copied out of a dictionary, and did this for several weeks; and then, when the editor ventured to point out that he did not want long lists of words but sentences and, if possible, sentences that formed an essay, I should fly into a rage and vow that I was unjustly treated and that some people did not know what they did want. I shall be told, of course, that domestic service is unpleasant, that the wages are poor, the work hard, and the conditions bad, and that any spirited and sensible girl would prefer to remain outside it and have her freedom. I have used this very argument myself. But I shall not use it again because it is twenty years out of date. If there are any houses where the conditions of service are still very bad and the servants' freedom is unjustly curtailed, they are probably the very large houses of the rich, and, ironically enough, these

Servants

are the very houses that servants prefer. There is a further irony in the fact that many servants, certainly the creatures of hate that have lately passed through these gates, do not take advantage of the freedom and the privileges they possess. Not only do they not want to work, but they do not want to make themselves comfortable and happy either. Living in the country as we do, we realized that it was a dull place for girls, and we made special plans so that they might amuse themselves both in the house and away from it. But these girls would not dream of becoming friendly human beings and amusing themselves; in this matter, apparently, they still believed in 'knowing their place'; and it was only so far as the work was concerned that they had determined to forget what their place was. They clung desperately to all the discomforts of domestic service.

Some people will tell you that it is all a question of 'class-consciousness'. Actually, however, to talk of 'classes' only complicates the tangle. There is nothing we should like better than the kind of servant one finds in France, who is extremely hard-working and loyal, but also independent and outspoken, not unlike a visiting aunt. She does not sulk in a corner, and then come out bowing and scraping, hating you not because she knows you want her to be servile, but because she thinks she ought to be servile to you and yet resents the fact. This seems to be the trouble now with servants in England. Their mothers were frankly servile, and their daughters will probably be frankly independent, but this generation, as oddly placed as this generation of masters and mistresses, will neither abandon itself to servility nor cut itself loose from it. Even the idlest, dirtiest, sulkiest, most ill-tempered of the girls we have had lately always answered me as if I were a being of another order and not merely a rather fussy but shy fellow-creature, who simply asked for so much service in return for wages, board and lodging. And because they compelled themselves to be docile and soft-spoken, they went away and disliked me and my family more than ever. They insist upon wearing uniforms, and then hate domestic service because they no long find themselves dressed in their ordinary clothes. Perhaps the secret of it all is that we are suffering for the sins of our fathers, for the old scraps of food, the miserable attic, the one half-day a week, the ' no followers ', the petty tyrannies of the great days of service. That is the only solution I can offer, and even that hardly explains why so many young women from the South Midland counties have lately passed through this house, making no attempt to do the work they offered to do and hating us all so strangely. Next week, it appears, we begin

Servants

again. We shall be at the station, hopefully waiting with the car, convinced that the luck must turn, representing, you might say, the whole human race.

SEEING STRATFORD

'YOU must admit you haven't been there,' they said. I told them I had been *through* the town more than once. But that was nothing, they retorted, because I hadn't *seen* anything there, didn't know where Shakespeare was born or buried or where Anne Hathaway lived, had never sat on the edge of the second-best bed. I told them I didn't care. 'We know you don't care for the sight-seeing part of it,' they confessed, 'but that won't last long. It's a delightful run, and look what a lovely morning it is.' And it *was* a lovely morning; spring in blue and gold; not the smallest pocket-handkerchief of cloud in the whole sky. Not only did I agree to visit Stratford-on-Avon but I also helped to take down the hood and the screens of the car, for apparently the moment had arrived for it to be converted into an open, summery affair. The five of us packed ourselves in, together with a great deal more lunch than we should ever require. Is there anything more terrifying to a person with sense and sensibility than a day's pleasure, what some people call a 'little jaunt'? The fuss and scurry and discomfort and egg sandwiches and dust and nipping winds—to be

Seeing Stratford

acquainted with these things is to prefer a day's work to a day's pleasure. Before we reached Stratford, the other two sitting at the back with me agreed that they never remembered a colder journey. It was very odd and very annoying. You appeared to be travelling through the very pomp of June itself ; the sky was a midsummer blue ; the roads shone in the bright sunshine ; you passed old men sucking at their pipes, sitting on the grass and wearing no overcoats ; and to the eye you seemed to be happily roasting in the golden oven of summer. But the cold was frightful. The wind, a dry north-easter, cut across the whole way, numbing our cheeks and making our chins really ache with cold. Yet whenever our watering eyes allowed us to see anything, there was the lovely lazy day spread in front of us. It was just as if we were bewitched.

The real literary shrine is, of course, a library. For the rest you may at times come close to an author's spirit in various odd places and atmospheres, it may be in an autumn wood, on a bare moor, in a bar-parlour, within sight of a palm reef and a line of breakers. But the official literary business, with its documents of birth, marriage and death, its museum and antique shop airs, its array of beds and pens and desks and chairs, its visitors' books and picture postcards and glib custodians, is simply so much solemn nonsense. The persons who

really enjoy this cultured and hushed-voice
sightseeing are never people who care very
much about books and authors. Stratford is
their Mecca. I hope Shakespeare himself knows
all about it, that he is keeping an immortal eye
on his birth-place. How he must enjoy the
fun ! I can hear him roaring with laughter.
I can see him bringing other immortals (probably Cervantes among them, for if those two
are not hand-in-glove, then there is no friendship
among the shades) to see the local branch of
the Midland Bank, which tries to look Elizabethan and romantic and even has some scenes
from the plays drearily depicted round its walls.
He will show them how everything in the place
is conscientiously thatched and beamed. He
will watch us paying our shillings in this place
and that to gape at an array of articles that
have really nothing to do with him, rooms full
of Garrick and Hathaway relics. His attitude
towards all solemn and pompous official persons
and bores was always touched with a light
malice and his own irony, and he must delight
in the fact that he contrived to leave behind
him so few facts about his life and so few things
to admire. He must enjoy watching his
biographers compiling their works, when they
know only too well—poor fellows—that all the
facts could be set down on two or three sheets
of notepaper and that they will have to write
page after page beginning, ' We can imagine

the young Shakespeare ' or ' No doubt the
poet at this time ' or ' Is it not likely that the
dramatist '—feverishly padding.

Having left little or nothing of his own behind
him, he must take a malicious pleasure in the
efforts of his townspeople to provide visitors
with Shakespeare museums. I hope he watched
them ransack every corner of the place and
dubiously install documents relating to the wood
of his mulberry tree and portraits of the mayor
of 1826. And I am sure he delights in some
of the custodians of these places. There is the
good lady—and very helpful and courteous she
is too—who repeats all the facts she knows in
a most fascinating whispering sing-song and
always ends every little speech with a comment
in exactly the same tone : I know that I could
have listened to her all day. Then there is the
man who has a passion for saying ' in the
summer months ', just as if the case were
entirely altered in winter. ' Here is a document
that interests a lot of people in the summer
months,' he told us ; and again : ' That's the
inspiration chair. In the summer months
ladies like to try it.'

We did not pay all the attention to him that
he deserved because we were obliged to keep
glancing out of the window. We were convinced that three men outside (and two of them
were undoubtedly Bardolph and Nym) were
wanting to steal our car. When we first drove

up to the place, they had approached us with some trumpery excuse, had indeed talked about taking photographs. Now amateur photographers and Shakespeare pilgrims are an innocent race, and these three, Nym and Bardolph and another, were very seedy and shifty-eyed. We waited for a few minutes, during which time they hung about suspiciously, vainly trying to look as if they were about to take a photograph any moment, and then at last we locked the car (a poor protection, I am told, against thieves), went in, and asked one of the curators to keep an eye on it for us. Naturally, however, we also kept an eye on it ourselves.

But what, it may be asked, were Nym and Bardolph doing there ? We soon found the answer, in a dense and dusty stream of cars and cycles and chars-a-bancs that passed us on the main road. The local races were on that afternoon, and Birmingham had descended upon the town. Perhaps Shakespeare himself might have been found up there, mingling sedately yet humorously with the crowd. I certainly caught sight of Ancient Pistol (in a bowler) hanging over the side of a char-a-banc. He was probably going to meet Falstaff (now haunting the ' silver ring '), who had no doubt suggested to friends Nym and Bardolph that a car might be ' conveyed '.

Yes, Shakespeare himself would laugh all

night if he spent a day in his little town now. He would be amused at the solemn arts and crafts persons who have set up shop in the kindly shadow of his great fame; at the expensive hotels that try to delude Missouri and California into the belief that they are hostelries lately removed from Eastcheap; at the Shakespeare This and the Hathaway That meeting the eye everywhere; at the transformation of his bustling little town into a shrine where Justice Shallow guides the feet and eyes of Judge K. Shallow. He would laugh but he would understand too. He would turn wise yet wondering eyes upon the little yellow man from Cathay who was looking down upon that flat tombstone in the old parish church. He would understand the middle-aged American woman (she had that curious dried look that comes to some American women and suggests they have been specially prepared for export, like dried fruit), who walked up to the curator of Anne Hathaway's cottage and cried: 'Well, I've had a lovely time in there and I wouldn't have missed a minute of it.' He would understand this, although he himself probably did not have a lovely time in that cottage. He would laugh but he would go down at once to the precious human stuff that is lying underneath all these solemn antics and mummery.

And there was one moment, the other afternoon, when I did really feel I was treading upon his own ground. It was when we were in the gardens of New Place, very brave in the spring sunlight. You could have played the outdoor scene of *Twelfth Night* in them without disturbing a leaf. There was the very sward for Viola and Sir Andrew. Down that paved path Olivia would come, like a great white peacock. Against that bank of flowers the figure of Maria would be seen, flitting like a starling. The little Knott Garden alone was worth the journey and nearer to Shakespeare than all the documents and chairs and monuments. It was a patterned blaze of tulips, the Elizabethan gentlefolk among flowers. The white ones, full open and very majestic, were the great ladies in their ruffs; and the multicoloured ones, in all their bravery of crimson and yellow, were the gentlemen in doublet and striped hose. The little crazy-paved paths added a touch of pride and fantasy and cross-gartering, as if Malvolio had once passed that way. And then, to crown all, there were tiny rows of sweet-smelling English herbs, thyme and sage and marjoram, and misty odorous borders of lavender. I remember that when we left that garden to see the place where Shakespeare was buried, it didn't seem to matter much. Why should it when we had just seen the place where he was still alive?

PHOTOGRAPHS

'I WOULD also recommend,' said the late Sir Walter Raleigh, talking of the Press, 'that a photograph of the author be placed at the head of every article. I have been saved from many bad novels by the helpful pictorial advertisements of modern publishers.' I delight in that remark just as I delight in its author (who has, I maintain, written the best letters of this century), but I hope there are not many of his way of thinking. If we are to be judged now by our photographs, there are some of us who will have to cast about for some other way of earning a living, for it is certain that writing will not keep us. To be judged by appearances, so long as what are called good looks are not demanded, does not alarm me. Anyhow, we all judge in this way daylong and cannot help it. But actual appearances give a man a chance ; there are the gleams and glints in the eye, the play of wrinkles, the antics of the mouth, all claiming attention ; and there is always something appealing about a rugged or vivacious ugliness. A photograph is another matter. I have never seen a photograph of anybody that made me want to know the

Apes and Angels

person caught grinning or scowling or gaping in it, for the camera has a trick of making humanity look either repulsive or insipid, except when it turns us into absolutely comic grotesques as remote from ordinary men and women as the figures of a Punch and Judy show. Consider the creatures who stare at us from the yellowed pages of the family albums. They are, it is true, old-fashioned and somewhat fantastic as to hair and whiskers and cravats, but then so are the people of the drawings of the period, and yet the strangest creatures we see above the signatures of Leech and Keene and du Maurier seem merely odd neighbours when compared with the monsters we see in the albums.

The worst drawing we have ever seen of ourselves, if we exclude the odd scribbles of people whose hand and eye are definitely alienated, has something in it that makes it preferable to the best photograph. Behind the camera there is no memory of how our faces move, and it can only see us as a momentary grouping of light and shadow. The artist is looking before and after as he sets down his portrait, and so he achieves, even in the sketchiest black-and-white, some suggestion of mobility and warmth. In the photograph everything is frozen. If the camera works quickly, as in a snapshot, our appearance during one fleeting moment is caught and

Photographs

fixed, with the result that it show us something our eyes have never really seen. We are trapped with an insane grin on our faces, it may be, or pinned against the background for ever in a monstrous attitude in which we could not possibly remain for more than two seconds. If the camera works slowly, moving along with time a little way, then we are asked to freeze ourselves. It is true we are generally told to 'look natural', but it is obviously impossible to look natural in such circumstances. Long before the two minutes have passed, the beautiful smile we put on has hardened into a ghastly grimace; we screw up our eyes to protect them from the glare of the lights; we can feel the veins beginning to stand out in our foreheads; and we know only too well that we are busy staging a burlesque of ourselves. The camera we confront on these occasions does its work very efficiently, recording with cruel precision every line and shadow of the idiotic face we have put on, a face that is a complete stranger to us.

I do not know which I dislike the more, these set 'portraits' or 'studies', the work of gentlemen with large studios and temperaments and cameras as big as packing cases, or the 'snaps' as some people, in their foul fashion, call them, those fantastic glimpses of oneself standing on the lawn or sitting in a deck-chair, gaping at nothing. More than once, when friends have been showing me photographs of groups of people, I have suddenly caught sight of a face that seemed strange to me, a face singularly vacuous or repulsive, and I have been on the point of crying out: 'Who on earth is that?' when it has dawned upon me sickeningly that that face was my own. I have never imagined myself to be a handsome man, and have even admitted, under pressure, that I am a trifle on the ugly side. But I have examined such snapshots, casual glimpses fixed for ever, with wonder darkening into despair. Surely, I told myself, I am not like *that*. Whatever I may have admitted on the subject of appearances, I have contrived to pass, in the secret councils of my mind, a tiny vote of confidence, on the ground that though I may not conform to certain rather absurd standards, nevertheless there is about my face a *something* that would be appreciated by the wise few. But when I have seen myself staring or grinning in those photographs, I have been compelled to take leave of vanity. So this is the thing that thinks itself so important and dreams its dreams and imagines that other people are interested and friendly or even affectionate! This is what people see and talk to and feed and sometimes cherish! For the space of several seconds I am humility itself.

I fare no better when the camera is leisurely in the 'portraits' and 'studies'. About once

Photographs

a month some photographer writes to suggest
that I should give him a sitting, being anxious,
he usually writes, to add yet another to his
series of portraits or studies of celebrities.
And let me say now that I cannot understand
why these photographers (Court Photographers,
too, some of them) should want my face. I am
clearly no beauty, so that no editor of an
illustrated weekly wants me to smirk at his
readers. I am so remote from any sort of
fashionable world that I should never be allowed
to pose even as a friend : Lady Woolworth,
Mrs. Revoke, Captain Bilker, and Friend ; not
even as that. As for being a celebrity, it is
absurd ; I am not yet even one of your tiny
little lions, roaring you as gently as any sucking
dove ; I am merely one of those young men
in baggy tweed suits who grumble to other
young men in baggy tweed suits that their
books do not sell, and are for ever telling one
another that other young men still, whose books
do sell and whose suits do not bag, are charla-
tans. For my own part, I should prefer the
photograph of any decent bull-terrier. However, such is the fact ; I am asked for a sitting ;
and the further fact is that I do not give a
sitting. But I will confess that in my time I
have given three, with intervals between of
despair and mounting hope. I do not remember
now whether these men called themselves Court
Photographers or Press Photographers. All

that I do remember is that they foolishly did it for nothing, that they tried to make me feel important, and that they succeeded in making me look like some one else.

The first photographer, very fashionable and obviously an indefatigable toucher-up, was clearly determined that I should be better-looking at all costs. The result was that he produced an elaborate portrait of a man who was obviously advertising a correspondence course in physical culture and was equally obviously a fraud. It was in this studio that I encountered the female secretary whose opening remark to me was : 'Now tell me all about yourself.' I wish I had told her that at least I had no intention of advertising a corre-spondence course in physical culture. Photo-grapher Number Two, who inhabited a gigantic studio full of guitars and shawls and cushions, and who was evidently highbrow, plumped me into a chair and switched on about ten search-lights, and afterwards produced an excellent likeness of a cleverish young Jew, on the make and quite unscrupulous. It took me two years or more to recover from that satanic trans-formation, but hope revived at last, and I agreed to visit a man who had done capital photographs of some of my fellow-writers, friends of mine. He was hearty and frank, and did not shrink from pointing out to me that a face like mine was hopeless unless it showed

Photographs

the camera a broad grin. So I grinned away,
and he dodged in and out of his black cloth.
A week afterwards I was shown half a dozen
different portraits of a fellow who looked as if
he travelled in wines and spirits during the
week, and was the life and soul of the West
Ham Dog Fanciers' Association every week-end,
the kind of man who is waggish with barmaids,
and who is referred to whenever you hear a
new arrival in a bar asking : ' Where's Charlie
to-night ? ' At first I could not understand
why my name had been written on the back
of all these photographs, so gross was the
transformation.

The truth is, there is malice in the camera
just as there is in all these clever modern
devices. It is as if the gods should overhear
our crowing : ' Another improvement ! Another
short-cut ! Another leap forward ! ' and then
give a nod to one of the company, who then
swiftly contrives that there shall be malice in
this new thing we have made. Thus there is
a sinister cast in the magic mirror we have
devised. It is indeed amazing that a visiting
friend, merely by pointing a black box at us and
making something click, should be able to catch
and retain our fleeting images, pluck out one
moment from the flux, so that people unborn
may possibly see the light and shadow that was
on our faces one summer morning. That
morning will be very distant then, will have

been whirled away farther than Sirius, will indeed be irretrievably lost, yet those people as they glance at the photographs will spend a second or so at our sides and so will have seen Time defeated. But it is all a cheat. The moment to which they will return will not be the moment we knew when we were facing the camera ; the foolish shadows grinning at them from a lost generation will be no true record but a cold libel, only tampering with their thought of us. That demure servant, the camera, will have had the last laugh.

A HOSTLESS VISIT

AT this very moment of writing we are having what seems to us a rather queer experience. We are guests without a host and hostess. The friends who had asked us to stay with them were called away the very evening before our arrival, and it was impossible for them to let us know because we had already set out on the two hundred and fifty mile journey to their house. They could only leave a message, imploring us to remain and make ourselves comfortable for the few days that must elapse before their return. We arrived two afternoons ago, and here we are, still making ourselves comfortable—hostless visitors. There would be nothing very odd about this situation if the house itself was an old acquaintance and its owners our old friends. But they are newish friends and this is our first visit here. Everything is strange, and though, after two days we have naturally come to be acquainted with these rooms and furniture and lawns and shrubberies, they still seem rather strange because we have not been introduced to them. If you are of my way of thinking, you will probably be convinced that this is an improvement upon the customary routine of country-house visiting, which involves so many introductions to things, so much initial sightseeing. No sooner are you in the house than the country host or hostess drags you out to look at the borders, the hot-house, the plantation, the domestic beasts, and for some reason always assumes that you have never seen any of these things before. I, who see nothing but processions of cows from my study windows at home, have been compelled more than once to leave my chair—and perhaps the first quiet pipe I have had all day—just to see the local cow. Who does not know that first afternoon and evening in the country, when, with aching feet and hot eyes, you are forced to stagger through a little hell of sightseeing?

Well, we escaped that, of course. There was nobody to show us anything, and we could begin by lounging about and gossiping and occasionally taking a peep at things when we were visited by a genuine little feeling of curiosity. We could poke about at leisure and were free for once from the grand tour. Moreover, when we did look at anything we could say what we liked about it. 'This water-colour's not bad.' 'What on earth made her put those hideous little china objects there!' 'This border's not as good as ours.' 'The carpet ruins this room.' 'Do you know, there's nothing in this bookcase but new American

A Hostless Visit

poetry. They can't possibly read the stuff.' I do not say that these are the actual remarks we made to one another, but we certainly made remarks of this kind. The difference between talking over a house without the owners being there and seeing it with them is the difference between reviewing a book and writing to thank an author for a presentation copy. Yet though we revelled in this new freedom, we found it was impossible to take full advantage of it. We were apparently at liberty to criticize the house as if it were a museum, yet actually we found that something restrained us. I noticed that whenever we found fault we lowered our voices, as if we were afraid our absent host and hostess would somehow hear us if we spoke up. Thus the gain in freedom of speech was not very great, and it has been more than counter-balanced by a definite loss of ease. It is very disquieting being a hostless visitor.

I am not very fond of staying in other people's houses at any time. It is true that their books and music and gardens and breakfasts always seem more exciting than one's own ; but then one is so seldom left alone to enjoy these things. I find the strain of being a visitor too great for me after about twelve hours. I cannot guarantee a smile and a word of praise at any time of the day. If I am left alone from breakfast until dinner, I can secrete enough sociability and politeness to carry me comfortably through the evening, but to be a smiler and a prattler first thing in the morning, when the liver is proclaiming that all is vanity and a weariness, is too much for me. Now here, of course, we have been free from all that, having neither host nor hostess nor fellow guests compelling us to be bright and chatty. This would seem to be the ideal form of visiting, of staying away from home. The best hotel could not offer such comfort and privacy, and there is no sightseeing or smiling chat or compulsory games. What more could the heart of man desire ? The question, as usual, is fatal ; and once more it does nothing but reveal the inevitable and colossal snag. What the heart of man chiefly desires is peace, and here there is none. It is impossible to be easy as a hostless guest, unless, as I suggested when I began, the house itself is an old acquaintance and its owners old friends.

Try as we may, we cannot escape the feeling of being mere interlopers. We move about calmly and even haughtily, but all the time we are terrified of the servants. We have never seen them before ; there is no master or mistress to interpret our wishes for us ; we do not feel that they are our paid attendants as we would if we were staying in an hotel ; and so we dare not give them an order, dare not meet their glance, and feel foolish as soon as they come near us. All this is very absurd, of course. There is no reason why we should not be at

A Hostless Visit

ease. Our friends have left instructions that we are to be well entertained until they return, and the servants themselves seem to be pleasant and obliging persons. The fact remains, however, that we are afraid of them and uncomfortable, though perhaps not so afraid nor so uncomfortable as we were at first. It is the same with the house itself. ' Now do, do make yourselves at home,' our host and hostess said in effect, and told us there was this and that and the other to amuse us, and even had a special wireless set sent up for us, a most fascinating affair that looks like a large wooden box (it is called ' portable ', though I should not like to ' port ' it more than two yards) but can bring noises from Paris or Aberdeen into the room. We know that our friends are anxious that we should treat the house as if it were our own, more especially as they were not able to be here to receive us. But not only do we find it impossible to treat the house as our own, we also find it impossible to regard it as the possession of a friend. We feel we have sneaked into it. Yesterday we seemed to walk about on tiptoe. Never have I spent a more restless day.

Everybody must know that restlessness which comes to the visitor who is left alone for a time (even if only for half an hour) in a strange house. Imagine, then, what we must have felt yesterday. We would go over to the book-shelves, taking out volume after volume (and sometimes hurriedly replacing them when we heard a noise behind us) but never reading more than a page or two, just as if we were in a bookshop. We would creep across to the music cabinet and guiltily pull out a drawer or so, find something that interested us, take it to the piano and then suddenly decide not to play it. There is a very good gramophone here, and yesterday I found some Cortot records and thought I should like to hear them. I tried two but could not listen in comfort. A Cortot record does not make a prodigious amount of noise, and yet somehow I felt that the gramophone was too obtrusive and was glad to turn it off and tiptoe away. I was fascinated by the wireless set (which for once had not any wires to be seen—it is rather queer that whenever we enter a room filled with wires we say, ' Ah, you've got a wireless '), which boasted an armoury of knobs, and I was longing to turn them round and round and hear what London and Bournemouth and Glasgow and the Eiffel Tower were saying. But after I had made a feeble little turn or two, my fellow interloper told me I would probably break it, and I was so alarmed that I shut it up at once. And never in my life have I felt so inquisitive as I do now. The whole house is full of drawers and cupboards that I want to open and explore. I creep about like Pandora herself. ' You'd

A Hostless Visit

like to look in here, wouldn't you ? ' a cupboard
sneers, as I pass. 'Well, you can't, you see.
You're wondering whether I'm full of tattered
copies of detective stories. Perhaps I am, but
it's no business of yours. You go to the
bookshelves and try to read the free verse of
Netta Natchett or the Imagist Poems of Hector
Isenbaum.' If we sit down, the arm-chairs
creak to one another : ' Who are these people ? '
Footsteps in the hall or above in the bedrooms,
say : ' Now what are they up to ? ' Every
time the gong sounds it cries : ' There's your
meal ready again. Bong, bong. I thought we
were in for a few easy days when the master
and mistress were called away. But no, *you*
must come here. Bong, bong.' I am writing
this essay on a little bureau in the drawing-
room, and it would be a much better piece of
work if the bureau did not keep muttering to
itself : ' Thinks he can turn the place into his
private study, does he ! He'll be looking in my
pigeon-holes for paper-fasteners next. Who
told him to come here, anyhow ? ' This makes
it difficult to settle down to the task of com-
position. Besides, I spend half my time, as I
sit here, looking over my shoulder. I do not
know what it is I expect to see, but it is something unpleasant. And I fancy that if we can
stick it out until our friends return—and
already there is some doubt about it—they will
find us unusually polite and complaisant visitors.

MR. PICKWICK RETURNS

THERE are, I know, any number of 'Green Dragons' in the land, but I wonder if you know the one I mean. It is no great distance from where I live, though actually it stands at the junction of two main roads, a few miles from the nearest village, in appealing isolation. It is, indeed, a noble old coaching house, brave yet with good beef and beer, old wood and shining pewter. There it lies in the very bottom of those green and grey saucers of rich country-side, for ever mellowed with haze, that are England herself. Once in that valley you must inevitably walk into the kindly maw of the 'Green Dragon'. Well, the other night, as I climbed the hill from Little Chanbury and dropped down through Long Moulford, I told myself there would be just time for a leisurely drink there before the place closed. It was the magical hour of dusk, of purple air and vaguely glimmering fields ; a time, you may say, when anything might happen. And when I had nearly reached the inn, something did happen. I saw a great shadow come stealing silently up the road, approaching the inn from the opposite direction. Clearly it was some kind of vehicle,

Mr. Pickwick Returns

but there was something curiously huge and ghostly about it. It came gliding on and I walked steadily forward, and it chanced that we arrived before the ' Green Dragon ' together. Now I saw that it was an enormous motor-coach, the largest I had ever seen. But the odd thing was that it showed no lights nor made any sound. Yet it was filled with people ; I could see rows of heads, a vague blur of faces through the dusk. It swung round in a lumbering yet spectral fashion and then stopped only a yard or two from where I was standing and staring. The light from the inn showed me a large device or monogram painted on the side of the coach. I made out the letters ' P.C.'.

There was not a sound, not another movement now, and as I stood staring there I began to feel creepy. ' Hello ! ' I cried, aloud. It was just as if the word had broken a spell. Instantly the coach was filled with bustling, bewildering life. The blurred rows of faces turned into very energetic people, who all stood up and began talking at once. I could not see them very clearly, but they appeared to be a most astonishing collection of persons, who looked as if they were returning from a pageant or a masquerade. Then above the babel I heard a voice that sounded strangely familiar. ' Sit down, old codger,' this voice cried. ' Sit down and keep still or you'll break your neck, as the church bell said to the vethercock.' It happened too that I caught the reply to this extraordinary command. 'Vy, Sammy,' said a husky voice, 'we're 'ere, an't we? And you're a-gettin' down yourself.' 'And what if I am, old 'un?' cried the first speaker. 'You keep still. I'm a-getting out to 'elp the Governor down. Your turn'll come, as the leg o' lamb said to the cab 'orse.' A moment later I saw an agile figure jump over the side, disappear for a second or so, and then return carrying some steps, down which a number of persons descended. The leader seemed to me a rather short, plump, elderly man, with a round face. He came nearer and I caught the flash of spectacles. 'This looks a capital inn,' I heard him declare to one of his companions. 'I think they might find room for us all here, what do you think?' Other voices chimed in now. 'A most beautiful night,' one of them murmured, 'when all Nature, except the lovelorn nightingale, seems asleep.' He might have continued in this strain, but he was interrupted by the fellow who had brought the steps: 'And the pike-keepers, sir. Don't forget them. They're not asleep, though p'raps you wouldn't say they vos part o' Natur.' 'That will do, Sam,' said the elderly gentleman. 'Mr. Snodgrass hasn't asked for your opinion.' Did this Sam then touch his hat and say, 'Sorry, sir'? I am not prepared to say that he actually did,

Mr. Pickwick Returns

for by this time I was lost in a maze of wonder
and the ground beneath my feet seemed to be
the shifting territory of dreams.

Other people had come crowding out of the
motor-coach, and could be dimly seen in the
dusk, stretching themselves and slapping one
another on the back. Everybody seemed to be
talking at once, but now and then I would hear
a voice that was raised above the general babble.
'Where's Bob Sawyer?' I heard somebody
cry, but I never discovered if he was there.
A thin young man, a very fantastic figure,
pushed his way through the crowd, looked up
at the inn sign, and was now addressing the
gentleman who seemed to be the leader of the
party. 'Stop here, eh?—just the place—know
it well—" Green Dragon "—plenty of bedrooms
—good beer—rounds of beef—apple tart and
Stilton—famous for 'em; I'll go in—tell 'em
who we are—big party—distinguished travellers
—special preparations—beds aired—supper on
the table—no waiting—best of everything—
otherwise business ruined for ever—shut up
shop—sold up—children in workhouse—do their
best and made for life—influential guests—
know a good inn—tell everybody—great opportunity for landlord—special terms—next week
crowded out—curious tourists—next year two
guineas a night—Americans come—fortune
made—retire for life—country gentleman—boys
at Oxford—girls at Court—happy ever after.'

Apes and Angels

When he had done, I heard that husky voice raised somewhere in the back of the throng. 'Wot did 'e say vos the name o' this 'ere public?' After having had the name repeated to him, the speaker called out: 'D'hear that, Sammy? "Green Dragon".' This Sammy, not without a touch of impatience, called back: 'Well, wot of it, old Nobs?' 'On'y this, Sammy,' the husky voice went on. 'I never knowed a "Green Dragon" yet as wasn't kept by a vidder and 'adn't a stuffed parrot in the tap.' This statement had reached the ears of the elderly spectacled gentleman near me, who cried: 'That's a most curious circumstance, Mr. Weller,' and seemed to be on the point of pulling out a large notebook when there was another interruption.

This came from a man in coloured glasses, who had fussily made his way to the front of the party. 'Bless my soul, Mr. Pickwick!' he cried. 'Are we staying here? And is this the "Green Dragon"? Do you know that I've never stayed at an inn of that name before? Isn't that extraordinary, really remarkable? You knew I was here, of course, one of the party? Magnus—Peter Magnus. Who's this, Mr. Pickwick? A friend of yours?' He was staring at me. They were all staring at me. Uncertainly, I moved forward a pace or two. 'Dear me,' said Mr. Pickwick, blinking at me. 'I can't say I remember this gentleman.' At that moment the thin young man, with the jerky manner of speech, came closer, and I thought he was about to shake my hand. 'Nonsense!' he said. 'Know him well—no strangers here—knows me too—Alfred Jingle, Esquire—come to welcome us—deputation of one—represents the county—deputy sheriff—going to read official address—got in left-hand coat pocket—pay attention—all ready for you, sir.' Mr. Pickwick turned to one of his companions, and whispered: 'I dare say Jingle's right. The news of our return here, after a hundred years, has reached these people.' He turned to me now. 'Well, sir, here we are, stopping for the first night of what you might call a centenary tour, for it's just a hundred years since we began our journey. Only now, of course, all our friends are with us, as you may see for yourself if you look around you. We are ready for you, sir.' Did they suppose I was about to give them an official welcome? Apparently they did, for there was neither a movement nor a sound now, and every face there was turned towards me. But how still, how ghostly they were!

'Here's that new chara of young Bardsley's,' cried a loud voice behind. 'Isn't it a size? Cost him something, that. Calls it the "Pickwick".' The inn was closing and men were coming out. There was the huge motor-coach, silvery in the queer half-light, but all the

Pickwickians had vanished. The man who had just spoken and one or two companions were looking curiously at the coach, and that was all. Where now were Mr. Pickwick, Tupman, Snodgrass, the two Wellers, Jingle and the rest ? Evidently the motor-coach was solid and real enough, though it was strange that it had come gliding up apparently without lights or driver. Perhaps my little dusk-dream, in which my old friends had returned so surprisingly, had begun the moment I set eyes on the vehicle, which had thus rolled straight through into my dream, shedding its lights and driver in the moment of transition. But what had Mr. Pickwick meant by his talk of a centenary ? I thought over these things as I walked home, still a little dazed, and it is hardly necessary to say that when I arrived there I immediately took out a copy of *Pickwick*. In the second chapter I read how the Pickwickians began their never-to-be-forgotten tour on 13th May 1827, and then I began to wonder if I had dreamt it after all.

VARIETY

THE only guardians of the domestic life and the domestic affections we have left seem to be the advertising people, who insist upon doing duty for the Lares and the Penates. They alone carry on the tradition of Dickens' Christmas stories, these crickets on the hearth. The more expensive the goods they praise, the louder they sing ' Home Sweet Home '. They like to buttonhole us about the ' wife and kiddies '. They believe we have such a passion for what they always call ' our own fireside ' that no matter what it is they have to sell, so long as it can be brought to the fireside, they believe we shall want it. Thus a pianolo gives us all the rich treasures of the world's greatest masterpieces of music at our own fireside ; and if that is not enough for us, then there is an encyclopaedia that will bring all the world's vast stores of knowledge to our own fireside. I have even seen a few desperate artists try to combine the motor-car with the fireside by showing the usual people in their arm-chairs and insinuating a tiny five-seater open tourer into the picture, where it rests on a dream fragment of road.

Apes and Angels

They tell us over and over again—it is their great opportunity—what wireless will do for us at our own fireside. Without stirring from our arm-chairs (for your good advertiser hates us to walk about or stand up) we can hear the news and the history of those deep depressions over Iceland, the very witty after-dinner speeches of politicians, descriptions of sonata-form and salmon tinning, jokes and jazz and music—and all delivered at our own fireside. This is indeed admirable, for even if you do not want to hear after-dinner speeches or dance bands (and I must say that both are insufferable when listened to, as it were, in cold blood) there is still the music. It is very pleasant to hear, as I did the other night, Miss Myra Hess playing her arrangement of that lovely chorale of Bach's, while sitting at home. No man in his senses likes the atmosphere of a concert-room, and nothing could be better at the fireside than good music.

Not everything, however, can be successfully brought to the fireside. I realized that the other night when I listened in to a variety programme. I have no fault at all to find with the programme itself. All the people were good of their kind, and their kind was that of the music-hall. They had better voices than the average music-hall singer, and I have no doubt that their jokes were really very good jokes. The band, which played bright jerky little tunes between the turns, quite in the old style, was really a better band than one ever found in the real music-hall. All that it was possible for man to do in such circumstances the B.B.C. and their performers did, and I beg them not to imagine that this is one of the usual complaints. Yet the fact remains that, to one listener at least, that entertainment seemed as dead as mutton, whole worlds away from the genuine variety show. What killed it was the fireside. It was just as if one had asked some racy fellow, encountered in a saloon bar, where he was in his glory, into the house and ushered him into the drawing-room, only to find that he was completely out of his element, not knowing what to say or where to look.

Nobody enjoys comedians more than I do, as my friends, who have been bored many an hour by my rhapsodies upon them, can testify, but I do not want a comedian—or at least another comedian, a professional—at my own fireside. It is one thing having those ridiculous swinging songs roared at you from the actual stage, with the drummer in the corner below banging away, and it is quite another thing to have them carefully telephoned to you, as you sit quietly and coolly at home, from the B.B.C. studio. You see the fish in its tank, a quick flash of colour in the green, a glitter of fin and tail ; but bring it out, into the biting air, and in a few moments it is nothing but a little greying thing, fading and stiffening into dead matter. So it is with the japes and antics and strummings and drummings of the variety show: they live only in their own atmosphere.

If the arm-chair I was sitting in, the other night, had suddenly narrowed and draped itself with the dingy plush of the three-and-sixpenny *fauteuil*, if the fire into which I was gaping had turned into a golden stage with the backcloth of some incredible marble hall, and the firebars and irons had become a dull blur of orchestra, if I had had a crowd of other humming and guffawing mortals on every side of me and the air had been thick with smoke and a vague smell of bottled beer, then I should have enjoyed that variety show. It would have been restored to its own atmosphere. I have always been fond of the Halls, though I suppose I am really too young to be allowed to write about them. I ought to leave that to those who remember the Halls when they had chairmen and whiskered lion comiques. Mine is a later era—and a provincial one at that—and such memories as I have are of little twice-nightly places and of Mark Sheridan and T. E. Dunville and Eugene Stratton and Florrie Forde and the Six Brothers Luck.

There were two music-halls in the town I lived in, and during my teens I used to go regularly

to one and to sneak off regularly to the other.
One was considered fairly respectable—even
deacons had been known to visit the place—but
the other, the one I sneaked to, was held to be
very low. And so it was, in one sense, for it
was almost underground, the gallery being only
level with the street. It was quite a descent
into the pit and the orchestra stalls (one
shilling). But the good people of the town—
the shop-and-chapel people, as a friend of mine
(we had bitter tongues in those days) called
them—regarded it as a still greater descent,
into Hell itself. One of the things that were
whispered about fellows who were obviously
going to the bad was that they were patrons of
the (shall we say?) Asterisk. The *demi-
monde* of the town were to be seen in those
orchestra stalls or lolling in the long bar underneath the stage, where you might sometimes
see the artistes themselves, glorious in grease-
paint. The Asterisk had an orchestra of ten,
I remember (I can see them now), and never
did ten men work so hard. The conductor
played a violin, beat time, nodded to his
friends, exchanged gags with the performers,
all without turning a hair. If there was the
slightest interval without music, those ten had
disappeared, and then were back, wiping their
mouths, before you could count twenty. There
was no nonsense about tuning up with them :
they scrambled in, picked up their instruments,

and were off at the first wave of the bow. They were always down on the programme to play an overture, and they always began one very loudly and at top speed, but they were never allowed to play more than a dozen bars before the curtain was up and they were on with something else. I do not suppose those ten men had the slightest idea what the second page of an overture was like or any notion of how to finish one. But they did their duty manfully and made more noise than any band I have ever heard since.

I liked the Empire—for that was the name of the more respectable Hall—but I liked the Asterisk even better. It did not pretend to be refined and to be fit for everybody. It was smoky and beery and noisy and vulgar, and if you did not like it, you could lump it or go across the way to the Mechanics' Institute, where, no doubt, a lecture entitled ' With Net and Camera on the Norfolk Broads ' was in progress. The Asterisk did not offer you feeble one-act comedies or solemn musical turns (in drawing-rooms with shaded lights) or imitation Russian dancing or gentlemanly entertainers at the piano. Indeed, if anybody at the Asterisk had tried to sing merely with a piano, had dismissed the magnificent ten below, he or she would have been hooted off. We liked to have the band with us, and the verse once and the chorus nineteen times. We were at once

Variety

noisy and critical, and in order to be pleased,
or even placated, we had to have artistes who
had stage personalities like a kick from a mule.
Half the stars of lighter stage in London to-day
would not have had a dog's chance at the
Asterisk, and rightly too. The stuff we were
given, I have no doubt, was poor enough,
nothing like so admirable in melody and wit as
the performance of the B.B.C. people the other
night ; but there, in that rich atmosphere, with
the stage glowing cavernously through the
blue haze, the drums rattling in your very ears,
it all seemed tremendously alive.

They tell me that variety is dying, that the
old twice-nightly Halls are being transformed
into either theatres or cinemas. If this is true,
it must be because variety has lost its own
unique atmosphere, its own sweet rowdy-
dowdy vulgarity, its mixture of silliness and
naughtiness, its Dear-old-pals and On-the-
spree-up-West airs—has, in short, been brought
closer to the fireside and so has faded and
shrivelled. I suspect too that, in the provinces
at least, the decay of puritanical manners, the
recent collapse of the shop-and-chapel front,
has helped to ruin the variety show. A good
part of its audience in my time was made up of
brisk lads who were defying the respectabilities
and ' seeing life '. You cannot see life through
a pair of ear-phones, and even the loudest loud
speaker does not make you feel that you are

rebelling against the minister and all his deacons. Merely to enter the old smelly passage of the Asterisk and plank down your shilling was an adventure. What, I wonder, are the adventures now?

THE STRANGE OUTFITTER

THIS morning I had a dream and the memory of it has been with me ever since, so that I feel already that I have had a tremendous day. I look back on the morning and see it stretching away, across two worlds, this one and another, wherever that outfitter's shop may be. I first opened my eyes, however, in this world. The room was full of sunlight, and I was sufficiently wakeful to wonder if it was late and then to look at my watch. It was three minutes past eight; I remember that distinctly. I don't remember how long I remained awake; all that I do know is that I dropped off to sleep again and that the next time I looked at my watch it was twenty minutes past eight. That wicked little extra sleep cannot have lasted longer than a quarter of an hour, but it lasted long enough for me to visit an outfitter's shop in some fantastic town of dreams. I have a vague idea that the adventures in that shop were only the concluding chapter of the dream, and that I had had a day or two's travelling, of the mysterious dream kind, very dark and crowded, before I ever decided to visit the Gent's Outfitter. But of

all that went before I can remember nothing
that is sufficiently distinct to be worth describing
so that my dream may be said to begin in the
shop. Once there, it is vivid enough. I have
not, however, the least idea why I had entered
the place at all. I may have gone there to
buy something or I may have walked in for
fun.

The shop was small and square, very cosy
and rather old-fashioned, the kind of establish-
ment you would find in a market town, a one-
man shop. It appeared to be lavishly stocked,
for all the walls were piled high with those flat
cardboard boxes (usually white with green
edges) that hold shirts and collars and ties and
braces and are so often lifted down and deftly
spread over the counter that they have the air
of being part of a juggling apparatus, first
cousins to those shining things that the attendants bring on to a variety stage. It had only
one window, which was small, rather low, and
looked out upon a wide street. There was
nothing remarkable about the place. We have
all visited dozens of shops like it, I imagine,
when we have been away from home, and have
discovered that we were in need of studs or
dress ties. The proprietor was not quite so
commonplace in his appearance. He was very
tall and thin, swarthy, with a large nose and
flashing teeth, but not a Jew, quite English.
He looked about forty. He was very much the

The Strange Outfitter

gentlemanly shopkeeper, dignified in black coat and striped trousers; without that unpleasant mixture of superiority and servility in his manner which is so common, and in its place a mingling of deference with a curious eagerness that was at once odd and attractive.

He wanted to mend the little straps at the back of my waistcoat. It didn't seem strange that he should know they were torn (they always are, for reasons that are now supposed to be discreditable); but I remember that I had no particular desire to have them mended. He insisted, however, and brought out needle and thread, saying that he could easily do it while I was wearing the waistcoat. We argued about this in an amiable fashion, and at last, finding that he was on the point of starting behind my back, I said that I would take off the waistcoat so that he could repair the straps at his ease. This I did and he helped me on with my coat again and I remained waistcoatless for the rest of the time. He sat down and presumably began stitching up the straps. I am not sure about this because I turned my back on him. Moreover, I never saw the waistcoat again.

'I think I'd like a cap,' I said, though why I cannot imagine.

'Caps? Certainly, sir. There you are,' he cried, but without stirring from his seat behind me. But there I was indeed, for the counter, right under my nose, was now heaped with caps. A moment before there had not been a single cap in sight. His voice came over my shoulder again : ' Nice lot of caps there, sir,' he was saying complacently. I cannot say they were a nice lot of caps, and I remember that I did not like the look of them at the time. They were all very large and loud and had enormous flaps, so that they appeared to have been designed for persons who were not sure whether to stalk a deer or attend a cup-tie. However, I looked them over and decided to try one on, singling out the nearest, a very woolly, ginger-coloured affair. There was a mirror at one end of the counter, and now, with the cap perched on my head, I turned to look at myself.

What I saw there rather astonished and—to be frank—delighted me. I had fine dark eyes, but all the rest of my face was dazzlingly fair. Not only was I handsome beyond the dreams of Hollywood, but I boasted a piquant kind of good looks, a contrast in colouring, not to be matched in this island. And, of course, the cap itself, which had worked the magic, looked admirable. I took it off and then a quick glance at the mirror showed me what I always see there, if not something a trifle worse ; so hastily donned the cap again and stared once more at that bright face, which seemed to have newly come from the mint of faces.

' I like this cap,' I told the man.

The Strange Outfitter

'They're very good caps,' he replied, still from somewhere behind my back.

'I'll take it then,' I said. I took it off, this time without another glance at the mirror, and put it down on the counter. The next moment there weren't any caps. I was just standing there, staring idly at the bare counter and puffing at a pipe.

'I'm sorry, sir,' said the man, who was now at my elbow, 'but there's no smoking in the shop.'

'Then you ought to have a notice of some kind,' I told him. I looked round the shop and waved my hand. 'You see, there's absolutely nothing here to tell me that smoking is not allowed.' I was very annoyed, but after a moment I quietened down and, pipe in hand, made him a long speech. 'The fact is,' I began, 'you don't understand my point of view. If I have once lit a pipe, I hate to leave it unfinished. I don't mind not smoking at all, if I know that I can't smoke, but it's annoying to light a pipe in the street outside and then to have to take it out in here.' There was a great deal more in this vein, I vaguely remember, all about the striking of matches and the taste of tobacco that is only half-smoked, and so on and so forth. I explored the subject very thoroughly. Meanwhile, I was not looking at the man himself but at the shelves and boxes in front. When I had concluded my speech, however, I turned to see how he was taking it, for he had been very quiet.

He had a pipe in his mouth, and was smoking it calmly and with every appearance of enjoyment. His eyes met mine without a trace of embarrassment.

'I thought you said there was no smoking allowed here,' I said.

'Not here,' he replied, puffing away. 'In the shop. There's no smoking in the shop.'

I looked round and then I understood what he meant. The shop had gone. We were still in the same place; there was the same low window and the same street outside; the room itself was neither larger nor smaller; but all the outfitting part of it, the counter and shelves and cardboard boxes, had vanished. It was now a little sitting-room, with panelled walls, an arm-chair or two, and a low settee under the window. I turned round and round examining the place, and seemed to lose sight of my companion. At last, however, while I was staring at something, with my back to the window, I heard a terrific chattering behind me.

The man was sitting on one end of the settee under the window, and on the other end was a very tall woman. Both of them were wearing huge masks. These masks were not unlike those worn by Indian witch-doctors. They seemed to be made of carved wood and were painted a bright red. The most surprising and

The Strange Outfitter

frightening thing about them, however, was that they had movable mouths. And now both mouths were opening and shutting prodigiously in a very rapid and loud and quite incoherent conversation. Neither the man, that once innocent-looking outfitter, nor his sinister companion took the slightest notice of me, and I stood there staring at them while they gibbered away at one another. Then I chanced to raise my eyes. There were crowds of people in the street outside, parading up and down, singing and dancing, and one and all of them wore masks. I saw none like the hideous pair in front of me, but nevertheless the whole strange town went masked. What did it mean? Where was I? I stared so hard that I stared myself out of the masquerade and the town altogether, into Oxfordshire at twenty past eight in the morning. I had been there and back in less than a quarter of an hour. But I wish I knew exactly where I had been.

I HAVE just finished reading a most fantastic book. It is called *The Chronicles of Osiris*, which chronicles, the sub-title tells us, are *Set down in the House of E. Eros-El Erua, they being male-female, born according to the laws governing the Dhuman-Adamic race, this being their fourth incarnation*. These chapters, we are told, were written down from clairaudient dictation, and they come, though not directly, from the Master Osiris : ' Messages are sent out to the material Earth, and are picked up by selected teachers functioning upon the different strata, each messenger passing it on until it reaches the physical plane.' What a pity it is that these works that have a superhuman agency behind them should be such poor stuff ! They only confirm our old suspicions that the universe is not on the side of good literature. There comes a voice from the great Beyond, the demigods or the Masters break their long silences, the starry runes are translated into words we can understand—and, alas ! we are reminded of nothing so much as our own familiar claptrap. If the universe cared about literature, these higher powers would

communicate with us in speeches that would make
Prospero's remarks after the revels or Milton's
complaint about his blindness seem like the idle
screaming and chattering of children. If they
themselves are indifferent to style and organization, the least they could do would be to enlist
the services of the now astral-bodied Shakespeare or Milton. It grieves me to think that
this Master Osiris, apparently one of the demigods of the solar system, should allow his
chronicles to be related in the style of the late
Rider Haggard at his worst. Moreover, his
chronicles reveal a dull, narrow, intolerant, and
completely prosaic mind. If this is the company we are to keep on higher planes, our fate
is horrible, the universe a nightmare of boredom.

He cannot complain of his subject, for you
could hardly have a better one. It is, briefly,
the destruction of Atlantis and the early history
of Egypt. I consider this magnificent material.
Imagine the vast stately narrative that Gibbon
would have made of it, in sentences like the
great Atlantic rollers that were the doom of that
strange continent. Or the thunder and lightning of Carlyle as he mocked and pitied the
hosts that ran screaming before fire and flood.
What a place our Mr. Wells could have made of
Atlantis in the days when his imagination ran
riot ! That lost continent has a fascination for
me. Now that the boy in me can no longer be
thrilled by the sight of blank spaces on the

map, I cling to the thought of Atlantis. We may or may not approve of those pleasant romantic persons, the Theosophists, but if we have any poetry in our souls we should be grateful to them for bringing to our notice the lost continents. I use the plural because not only have they restored Atlantis to the world's history, but they have discovered a still earlier and larger continent called Lemuria. In this volume I have before me there is a map of the world in which both Atlantis and Lemuria are back in their places. Atlantis is an island rather larger than India neatly dropped into the very middle of the Atlantic. Lemuria is in the Pacific and is a colossal island about six times as big as Australia. This map gives me a little thrill every time I glance at it. I notice the familiar coast-lines, where there are wireless stations and newspapers and jazz records and communist meetings, and then suddenly my eye is caught by these two strange shapes in the Atlantic and the Pacific and wonder is born again :

> What poets sang in Atlantis ? Who can tell
> The epics of Atlantis or their names ?

Not I, for one. Nor am I sorry.

I first read about Lemuria, that land of ghosts, in some vast Theosophical history of mankind that was good nightmarish reading.

Atlantis

I cannot remember much about it now, but I
know that it pre-dated Atlantis itself and came
in time to be an evil continent and so was
destroyed. Nearly all our legendary monsters
—the Cyclops, for example—are nothing but
imperfect recollections of various Lemurians,
probably of our former acquaintance. You have
only to look at the place on the map, a colossal
squat thing taking up most of the Pacific, to
see that it must have been a horror. I picture
it vaguely as a place of mud and mist and
monsters, though Master Osiris tells me that
its people (if they were not too Lemurian to be
called people) practised black magic, and were
given to celebrating abominable rites, so it is
possible they were highly—in fact, too highly—
civilized. Well, they perished, they and all
their works ; the earth split and sent up tongues
of fire, the sea came rolling in, and nothing
remained. But a few of the chosen were led—
in boats, I take it, right round the Horn,
though they may have had flying machines
for all we know to the contrary—to the green
isle (I will swear it was green) of Atlantis.
What happened there ? Master Osiris tells us
very little ; he is too busy, describing with
what looks suspiciously like complacent egoism,
the Temple on the Sacred Heights, ' situated in
the heart of the high mountains beyond the
tablelands and inaccessible to those who knew
not the power of levitation'. There was, we

gather, a long conflict between black magic and white magic, ending at last in the total destruction of the continent and an exodus of the chosen to such astonishingly familiar places as Egypt and Greece ; but that is all we know, or at least all I know. I do not want to know any more. My imagination can do the rest, and is only too glad of the opportunity of having a whole blank continent and thousands and thousands of years of human history to play with. In odd moments, thrusting aside Europe, America, Asia and Africa (I never trouble myself about Australasia), I brood over our lost Atlantis.

History only goes back a few thousand years at the most and even then it is misty with legend. On the other hand, we are told that man has been prowling about this planet for hundreds of thousands of years. What was he doing all that time ? It is always assumed that he was wandering about naked or dressed in skins and living a very spare life in caves and dug-outs. We call him prehistoric ; make him very shaggy, give him a club, and have done with him. But what reason have we to suppose that he was like this for about a hundred thousand years ? All the evidence is against such a supposition. Three thousand years ago the inhabitants of this island were savages, and now they labour in vitriol works or coal mines, draw dividends and go to cabarets, and are as civilized as education and Sunday newspapers can make them. Are we to believe that nothing of this kind ever happened during the ninety-seven thousand years that went before ? Why, when we bear in mind these huge flights of time, the original Sphinx and the Cenotaph in Whitehall are more or less contemporaries, and Birmingham rises as soon as Babylon decays. Our civilization is merely an affair of to-day and yesterday. There has been time enough for half a dozen such civilizations to flower and fade.

It will be said that we have no evidence of their existence. People forget, however, that the evidences of a high civilization are frequently the flimsiest of things that could not withstand the wind and weather of a hundred years, let alone some gigantic catastrophe and the dust and rain of ten thousand years. The man who lived in a cave some forty centuries ago is able to leave behind his tools and his art gallery as enduring witnesses. But what can Mr. Smith, Acacia Villas, Streatham, with his gim-crack house, his little wireless set and gramophone, his foolish sticks of furniture, leave behind to mark his passing ? The ink is rotting the pages of his books at this very moment and in fifty years they will be shredded away. Suppose the earth beneath us suddenly begins to rock, spouts fire and poisonous fumes, and the Atlantic sends a fifty feet wall of water rushing over us, what happens then to the B.B.C., or the Cavendish Laboratory at Cambridge, the works of Armstrong Whitworth or the teashops of J. Lyons ? In twenty thousand years' time we should be the vaguest of legends, known only to poets and theosophists. And the poets would only remember this fantastic Europe so that they might brighten a line in some verses that describe the pains and pleasures of their love ; and the theosophists— or whatever they will call themselves then—will only drag us into some priggish and lying fable.

I have no doubt that Atlantis once was, and that a civilization, probably infinitely more sure and subtle than ours, once flourished there. It is possible that the most astonishing of our feats would seem very clumsy and childish performances to the Atlanteans, who once lived, gravely but sweetly, in towering white palaces, looked out over the foam of the Atlantic, and talked in soft voices of the destiny of man. Perhaps all our legends of some place of happiness in the Western Sea, of the Isles of the Blest, the Fortunate Islands, the Isle of Seven Cities, that Avalon where there is neither rain nor snow and unfading apple-blossoms brighten the air, are only the last rumour and remembrance of Atlantis. Where the liners go churning on their way and the little tramp steamers shiver in the green troughs, fathoms below the cotton-brokers playing bridge in the

Atlantis

smoke-room and the girls flirting in the lounge
and the stewards drinking bottled stout with
the cook in the galley, there lie in the darkness
and the utter silence of the deep seas, the fallen
white palaces of Atlantis, once so bravely
pointing to the stars. We shall do well to
remember this lost continent. If it were
restored to the map of the world, along with its
ghostly sister, Lemuria, we might even yet
learn humility from the atlas.

THE SCHOOL MAGAZINE

THAT we have not lately turned some fantastic corner but are still moving along the same broad road, that boys are still boys and schoolmasters still schoolmasters, that, indeed, life changes very little, all these things are to me amply proved by the copy of the School Magazine I have just been looking through, the fond trivial record of the Summer Term. Sometimes I imagine that everything is in a kaleidoscope, that we are all being 'translated', and that if, for example, I returned to my old school, whose magazine this is, I should find that it was all different, the masters all cranks, and the boys all solemn little horrors. The Magazine—and this is the first copy of it that has come my way for many a year—reassures me, not merely as to this particular school, but as to all other schools (barring a few freakish establishments) and their boys and masters, and, leading out from them, English life in general. It is true there are differences, for the world must wag. Thus, I am told that on Friday, May 27, 'the Upper School had the pleasure of hearing a lecture on Debussy, the French composer'. In my time we had not

The School Magazine

arrived at Debussy, though we of the Upper School listened with the same sort of pleasure to similar lectures. I suppose that in twenty years' time the subject will be Stravinsky (who seems to me just bearable), and that twenty years after that, when you and I are either dead or blind, deaf and silly, the lecture will be on some composer, probably Chinese or Arabian, whose work would seem to us so outrageous that we should run screaming from any performance of his works. Nevertheless, I know what the Upper School will think of him ; they will vote him a bore, but will still be found, in the tactful columns of the magazine, having the pleasure of hearing the lecture.

Such a difference, it is obvious, is nothing more than a mere change of neckties. As I turn page after page, I go back to a world I seem to know far better than I do any world into which I have penetrated since, so unchanging that I see it now as if it were a tableau. And this record of it seems identical with those that you and I remember. The monthlies, the weekly Reviews, the newspapers, they are all very different from what they were when we were chewing our wooden pen-holders or drawing whiskered faces in the margins of our exercise books, but the School Magazine is the very same we knew then. It lies before me now in all that hideousness of shiny paper and sprawling type which is so familiar. That old-fashioned format lives on in these productions, just as mid-Victorian drawing-rooms contrive to live on in the lounges of little country hotels. Thus it is that the appearance of these magazines changes not at all, so that they have only to catch our eye to command our memory. So, too, the matter and the manner are the same as ever. My first impulse was to find that feature of the paper which is the refuge and stand-by of all hard-pressed editors the world over, that feature which may be found in all school and college magazines, and in all those periodicals that do not ask their readers to be anything but guffawing boys. I refer, of course, to the page of little-jokes-by-people-in-the-know, the page that is so easily edited. If I had not found that page I should have been a lost man; the very ground would have been cut from under my feet; I should have been compelled to admit that time had flown too fast for me. But it was there, secure in the middle of the Magazine. In my time, I think, the paragraphs began with IF, but now they begin with THAT; and those who delight in revolutions may make the most of the change, for I can find no other. Let us have a paragraph or two, for old times' sake :

THAT certain eminent members of the Sixth have been studying their geological trees.

THAT, according to a Transitus youth, a centurion is a man who has lived a hundred years.

THAT a certain Physics master has begun to study Welsh.

The School Magazine

You have to be behind the scenes to appreciate the full force of these thrusts, and we—alas !—are a long way from being behind the scenes now ; but the time has been when we were there too and guffawed and nudged one another over this page, that is, when we did not vote it ' rotten ' and ' putrid '.

All the other features are here. There is the usual essay (this time *Easter in Paris*) that opens with such dash (' Paris, wonderful city of our imagination, city of marvellous buildings ', etc.), and gradually droops (' Of course, we feel we could have spent weeks enjoying the beautiful and well-known masterpieces in the Louvre ' —a lie if there ever was one !), and at last drearily trails (with such remarks as ' The French people themselves provided a never-failing source of interest ') to the end of the page, where we can see the author throwing down his bitten pen and dashing out into the sunshine. There is the usual burlesque in blank verse : *The Stolen Trophy* (*A Tense Drama in Two Thrilling Throbs*) :

> Indeed, I thank thee, dame,
> For thy compassion, which I sorely need.
> Thrice hath the melancholy onion shed its leaves,
> Thrice hath asparagus turned to mouldy grey,
> Since I first gazed into my Hilda's eyes.

And, of course, the usual little satirical things, the sharpening of wits against the world's whetstone. One of these describes that anti-climax (the very symbol of life), the Picnic. The author ruthlessly presents us with a picture of the early morning bustle, after which : ' By eleven o'clock we all were packed tightly in a 'bus, holding firmly on to our paraphernalia, and with a look of grim determination on our faces. We meant to have a good time. When we alighted from the 'bus we found ourselves on a stony road, along which we walked for miles. No one seemed to have the slightest idea where we were going ; we merely staggered on and on in the blazing sun.' After that the description of the mournful lunch, the discovery that no records had been brought for the gramophone, and the final downpour of rain, forceful though that description is, need not be quoted, being itself an anti-climax after the passage above. But of those few sentences I have quoted, I will say this, that there are innumerable adult authors, who may be found in *Who's Who* and the Royal Society of Literature and have been living comfortably on their royalties for years, who have never in their lives written a short passage that threw such a strong clear light on things as they are. If I had a commonplace book, that passage would go down in it at once, and people would imagine it was a speech by a Tchekhov character.

The Editorial is the same as ever, being

The School Magazine

obviously written by a master who was, like
most schoolmasters, torn between the desire to
be helpful and the desire to go away, miles and
miles away, and never see a boy again. After
quoting three indifferent lines, it begins :
'Thus does the poet Coleridge denounce the
non-combatants in sporting activities.' It con-
cludes with these remarks : 'The efforts of
contributors are sometimes severely criticized
by persons who have never contributed anything. Our School Magazine has always been
regarded as a splendid production, and we feel
sure that no member of the School would wish
it to belie its reputation.' And that's that,
you can hear the honest man saying, as he
pushes the paper away and lights his pipe.
Here, too, are the notes, the same old notes.
The Debating Society is with us again, and we
learn how on the subject, *That books have a
greater influence on character than friendship*,
' all spoke confidently and convincingly ', and
that later when the subject was, *That the
demands of convention are tyrannical*, 'greater
controversy was manifest, and a heated dis-
cussion ensued ', and we know how many *ums*
and *ers* and desperate jokes and lame conclusions
are concealed behind these large and friendly
phrases.

Passing on—as the lecturers with lantern
slides always say—we learn too that 'The
Photographic Society has not been as successful

this year as in former years, but with fewer members some good work has been done.' Was ever a Photographic Society as successful this year as last year ? No, it is not in the nature of such a society to be, but nevertheless it always does good work ; we never remember it when it was not doing good work ; though probably our only recollections of it—never having been members ourselves—are nothing but a remembered glimpse of certain mild and spectacled youths peering at negatives together.

In the House Notes, of course, there is some straight talking. There is always one House that stays at the bottom in everything, and that does not care, being filled with boys who are not bright and obedient and energetic, but are impudent loafers. (Being a safe distance from any school and the duty of teaching the young, I can afford to declare that these are the boys I like best.) This House is as usual addressed with some sternness : ' In the previous term's House Notes we said that our position called for some straight talking. This time you are going to get that talking. Poor in school, mediocre in sport——' But there, we need not go on, for we have all had our straight talking and do not want any more. There is nobody now to tell us that we are poor in school and mediocre in sport (though it is as true as ever), and that at least is a gain ;

The School Magazine

though if there were, we should be back again in the vivid and surging life that is there behind these stiff little magazine notes, surprised to find how bright the fields were in the sunlight.

INSECTS

NOW that the swallows and the nightingales,
the laburnum and the lilac, are with us,
so too are the insects. In my study, which
was once a loft above an old dairy in the garden,
fat wood lice creep about ponderously like grey
short-sighted old gentlemen. Bees and wasps
have begun to fly in through the open windows
and keep up a furious buzzing among my books.
I have seen a centipede or two. What a
creature this is !—an inch of nightmare. Last
night some cockchafers came winging into the
drawing-room and were so like bullets that
you might have thought Nature was standing
outside in the garden taking aim at us with an
old-fashioned musket. Only yesterday afternoon, I followed the bidding of the moralist and
went to the ant. I was lying down on the lawn
—on the far and very rough side, let it be said—
watching a colony of them running about,
trying to understand what tasks kept them so
feverishly busy. But I never found out what
they were doing ; they merely ran and ran and
only stopped now and again to exchange a
word, or the equivalent of a word in ant life,
with their fellow-labourers. I have no doubt,

Insects

however, that they were all doing something, and do not feel disposed to agree with Mark Twain, who declared that the ant was a fraud. After all, if some creature as big as a hill, a being that lived for two thousand years, watched us throughout one of our mornings (about three minutes of his time), he would never be able to understand why we were all so frantically busy, what it was that kept us popping in and out of buildings and scurrying down streets. It can seem futile even to us ourselves, so we can easily imagine what so large and leisurely a creature would think of it.

Then there are the spiders. They are most in evidence here about August, but even now we seem to discover more and more of them every week, little ones that go swinging out into mid-air on the end of their own silken ropes, thin ones with tiny bodies and long legs that race down walls, and fat hairy ones that pretend to be dead and are obviously wickedness itself. These last terrify all the womenfolk here, and indeed all the women who come visiting here. I do not share their horror of spiders, and may be seen on many an evening dealing roundly with the insects. Perhaps, however, I ought to say that I am not afraid of English spiders, because I once saw a spider that made me feel very uncomfortable. I saw it on the quay at Port Limon, a little gaily-coloured and cosmopolitan town in Costa Rica that looks as if it had been invented by O. Henry. Port Limon spends most of its working hours loading ships with bananas, and apparently this monstrous spider had hidden itself among the fruit. There are stories of these horrors travelling to England and suddenly revealing themselves to Covent Garden porters. I had heard those stories before and had always found them difficult to believe, but once I had seen that spider the difficulty was removed. If a Covent Garden porter finds himself charged with being drunk and disorderly, he ought to hint to the magistrate that he had spent a few minutes of the previous morning looking into the eyes of one of those tropical spiders, peering at him over a bunch of bananas. A nigger who was hanging about the quay, I remember, told us that the spider we saw there was not a creditable specimen. ' Him little one,' he observed blandly. ' You should see him grand-fadder.' He should have said ' grandmother,' I believe, because the females in this kind vastly outgrow the males, whom they commonly kill and eat. I can imagine few experiences more hair-raising than a sudden and unexpected encounter with that spider's grandmother. She must be as big as a tureen, as hairy as a sweeping brush, and as malevolent as the devil himself. Let us be thankful that she is crouching some-where in the hot swamps of Central America and not putting the first of her thick hairy legs over the window-sill in our drawing-room.

Thus it is that though I do not share my household's terror of the spiders that visit us, I can quite understand it. It is only that, being more insensitive than they are, I need a larger size of spider to impress me. Our attitude towards these creatures is very curious. There is obviously no material reason for our dislike of them. Spiders do not pilfer and soil our food as rats and mice do; they do not, so far as I know, bring any disease into our homes; and they prey upon such insects as flies, things that are at best a nuisance and at their worst a real danger. We ought to be pleased to see spiders so long as they do not attain to a size that enables them to give us a good hard bite. We ought to regard them as clean and useful little creatures, humble friends of the family, and should be ready to pet them and admire their astonishing habits. Why do they fill us with loathing? Why do we point to them shudderingly and then murder them? Is thy servant a fly that she should do this thing? It is all very curious. Those large house-spiders, it is true, outrage decency in the matter of the number and the hairiness of their legs, and most women of my acquaintance declare that there is something terrifying or sickening in the very sight of these creatures on the move, racing along the wall. But after all they are only running away, taking their hairy legs and blood-sodden bodies as far as possible from the nearest human. If they always scurried towards the most shrinking woman's nose, there might be some sense in the outcry against them. Let us admit that our attitude is unreasonable.

It is, I think, the idea of a spider that really works the mischief in us. The thing has come to be accepted as a symbol of whatever is predatory and sinister. Its ingenuity is too devilish to be admired. It can be matched, however, over and over again in its own world, a world that seems to most of us absolutely repulsive, appalling. Only the man of science can wander about at his ease in that world of insects. He can do it because he is only in search of curious information and knows there is plenty to be found there. You can hear him declaring : ‘In all centipedes, except *Scutigera*, respiration is effected by chitinized tracheal tubes which extend with their ramifications throughout the body and open to the exterior by means of spiracles perforating the lateral or pleural membrane of more or fewer of the somites below the edge of the terga.’ He is cool but interested because the creature is lying dead in front of his eyes, which now see it as a piece of mechanism. He is at ease in the world of the insects because he has turned it into a museum, a collection of mechanisms, all to be examined and reported on at leisure. But if

Insects

you spy upon it as an arena of life, as another ring in the great circus, you are filled with horror. These are such stuff as nightmares are made on. We have only to stoop and use a magnifying glass to imagine ourselves in hell. Fiends would be proud to wear such shapes. When Mr. Wells took us to the moon and wanted to show us moonish creatures, he had only to enlarge a few specimens from the nearest ant-hill to capture our imagination and leave us fascinated and appalled. Here under our feet is a grotesque and bitter travesty of life. The sluggard goes to the ant and thereafter determines never to raise a hand again. If there is a death in the house, we tell the bees ; but when the bees do the telling, there is also a death in the house, the death of all our hopes. Here, in the hive, is the completely efficient and orderly society, the reformer's dream, our goal in miniature, and it seems a dreary horror.

Compared with the blustering mammals, all these tiny creatures, so cool and ingenious in their efforts to feed and reproduce themselves, seem to be very ancient and wise inhabitants of this globe. They have successfully solved problems that we ourselves have not yet solved. It is true that we seem to have certain advantages. No beetle has yet been discovered standing before the carcass of a man, lecturing upon it to other beetles. But then we should not know what was happening if we did come upon the scene. There may, for all we know to the contrary, be philosopher ants, and a turn of the spade in the garden may put an end to theories of reality that would command our respect if we could but understand them. The bees may have come to the conclusion that any scheme of life that does not concentrate entirely upon the production of honey and more bees is wasteful and futile, Perhaps all the drones are artists and philosophers. The spider that scurries away at a touch may be thinking that the large two-legged creatures will not last much longer but will soon join the ichthyosaurus and the pterodactyl. Such reports as we have, however, suggest that nothing of this kind is happening and that the insects feed and reproduce themselves with a blind cunning and have no time for poetry and philosophy and fun. And that, I suggest, is why the idea of them frightens or depresses us, why we find it difficult to give them a place in our brotherhood under the stars. Earth, our parent, who wants all the poetry and philosophy and fun she can get, tried her hand on the insects, but when they failed her she left them to their own cold and dreary devices. Since then she has tried her hand on us, and is indeed still trying, and sometimes she is satisfied with our progress and at other times she is not. Just now—but there, let us think about the bees and the ants and the spiders.

A LONDON HOTEL

WE are staying in an hotel in one of those squares at the back of Oxford Street. You will say that we ought to have more sense, but we have our excuses. We had to come up suddenly; the rooms we usually have were engaged; we were told that this was a good hotel. It is one of those hotels that like to describe themselves as quiet places for gentlefolk. They are, I believe, a distinct type. They have no bands nor dancing nor cocktail bars; they do not advertise themselves in the illustrated weeklies; they are not very expensive but neither are they very cheap; and they maintain, very firmly and consistently, a fairly high standard of inconvenience and discomfort. They occupy a middle position between those dreary bed-and-breakfast warrens that are always near the big railway stations, so that provincial noncomformist parsons may dive into them five minutes after giving up their tickets, and those palatial hostels where innumerable page-boys may be seen flitting above ten-pile carpets, carrying Martinis and the *Chicago Tribune*, places indeed that the likes of me only visit in the company of American publishers. There must be scores of hotels of this middle kind in London. I have stayed at a round dozen of them myself, probably more, for I have never stayed twice at the same one : I am not such a fool as that ; but nevertheless I am fool enough to imagine at times that I shall stumble upon one that is really different from the others. If possible, however, I try to make other arrangements : my optimism has reasonable bounds.

Here we are, then. Once more we are quiet dignified gentlefolk staying at a quiet dignified hotel. My room is more fantastic than usual. It has all the appearance of having been at some time a corridor, though possibly it is really a section of what was once an immense drawing-room. Whatever it was, it is now an extraordinarily, inhumanly long and narrow apartment, a place ripe for a German film producer. At one end is a long narrow window and at the other is a long narrow wardrobe, which has a mirror that always offers me a monstrous distortion of myself, who appear in it as if I were fully as broad as I am tall. This is, of course, an obvious optical illusion, but it adds nothing to my pleasure. It is quite impossible to have a night's sleep in this room, which must have been designed by some one who either never slept or never did anything else. Over the door is a large fanlight that is brilliantly illuminated all night because the

A London Hotel

lights in the corridor outside are never turned
out. (They will be to-night, however, even if
the bodies of the night-porter and the Boots are
found afterwards near the switch.) There is
no escaping this illuminated fanlight once you
are in bed, and no doubt advertising people will
soon take advantage of the fact. But that is
not all. This room is on the first floor, just
above the main door of the hotel, and my pillow
is not more than a yard from the window,
through which all the noises of the street, taxis
starting up and hooting away, come at all hours.
For two nights now this room has offered me
glimpses of eternity. It is determined to make a
thoughtful man of me. Mere reading will not
do. The electric light is so placed that you can
only read at the cost of having smarting eyes.
Moreover, when you have read yourself into
feeling sleepy again, you must then get up to
turn out the light, with the result that you are
wakeful once more. If any man wishes to
know what he thinks about life at quarter to
three in the morning, let him occupy this room
for a few nights.

The only meal we are taking in this hotel is,
of course, breakfast. There is something very
queer about these London hotel breakfasts.
Everything seems to be there, porridge, fish,
sausage, kidney, eggs and bacon, toast and
marmalade, tea and coffee. These viands are
not merely names on the menu but solid bodies

set on the table for you to eat. You may
spend twenty minutes disposing of them. Yet
there is a curious unreality about these meals.
They are like those dinners that actors pretend
to eat in the second act of comedies. At the
end of them, you feel you have had enough,
indeed more than enough, but you cannot help
suspecting that you have only been playing a
trick on your interior and that the trick has not
quite succeeded. These sausages and eggs and
bacon are somehow not real sausages and eggs
and bacon ; they are not the things in themselves, but mere appearances, part of some
phantasmagoria of the kitchen. It is all like
eating food in a dream. And the waiters
themselves are in the secret. There is mockery
in the gusto with which they set before you
these spectral eggs and rashers. I have never
been one of those members of the audience who
go on to the stage to keep an eye on the conjurer, but I fancy such people must have the
same sensation I have when I am breakfasting
in this fashion. Those liquids that the conjurer
pours out of his magic kettle—I will wager that
they taste exactly like hotel tea and coffee.
Possibly these are conjurers' eggs, coming not
from a hen but a hat. And the waiters *know*,
of that I am certain. That is why the younger
ones can hardly keep a straight face.

The head waiters are grave enough, but they
are also sinister. I have noticed that time after

A London Hotel

time. The head waiter here, for example, could walk straight into a mystery play and be worth fifteen pounds a performance as a collector of suspicions. He has a villainous bald front, a crooked nose, and deep-set but quite colourless eyes, and you could swear that he had disposed of the body only five minutes before he walked into the dining-room.

There is a room here asking for a murder. It is one of the three lounges. The first lounge is to the right of the entrance hall, and is always full of middle-aged Scotswomen playing bridge. (Why are these hotels always full of middle-aged Scotswomen ?) The second lounge is to the left of the entrance hall, and is a leathery, railway-guide-and-illustrated-paper sort of place. One end of it is always occupied by young wives sitting up very stiffly and waiting for their husbands, who are at the telephones asking if Mr. Murchison will be in or telling somebody that they can offer 2,500 at $3\frac{3}{4}$. The other end appears to have been annexed by a man with a vaguely military appearance, who yawns a great deal but contrives to look as if he has only to have two more to be tipsy. It is the third lounge, at the far end of the entrance hall, that is ripe for a murder. It is much bigger than the others but hardly used at all.

Yesterday, I happened to be in the hotel about half-past four, and so ordered tea. After waiting about ten minutes, I asked the waiter where it was. 'I've put it in the Brown Lounge for you, sir,' he said, and then it was that I discovered this mysterious room at the end of the hall. It was closely shuttered and very dimly lit, full of enormous chairs and settees, and there were dim acres of engravings and photogravures on the walls. I groped my way to a very large chair and a very little table with a tray on it. The only other people there were two old women who talked in whispers; and if one of them had turned out to be Dickens' Miss Havisham I should not have been surprised. All the noises of the hotel and the streets outside were banished with the closing of the door, and there was no sound at all but the vague whispering of these two old women. Usually I linger over tea, but yesterday there was no lingering. It seemed like eating bread-and-butter in a mausoleum. If ever I want to murder a man, I shall take him in there.

I can see the whole thing. I shall pretend that I want to have a quiet chat with my victim and shall suggest coming to this hotel for tea. As soon as we arrive, I shall seek out the head waiter, that sinister figure. 'I want tea for two,' I shall tell him, softly but with the right emphasis. 'Ah, tea for two,' he will say, looking at me with those colourless eyes. 'The Brown Lounge?' There will be a kind of cold flicker in those eyes. 'Yes,' I shall reply, **very**

A London Hotel

softly. 'The Brown Lounge. Tea for two.
And a sharp knife.' Then I shall rejoin my
man, and, talking very loudly and cheerfully,
with many a clap on the back, I shall march
him down the hall and into that shuttered room.
'Rather a dreary sort of hole this, isn't it?'
he will say, staring about him. 'Not a bit of
it,' I shall reply. 'Just a quiet hotel for
gentlefolk, that's all.' The head waiter himself,
I trust, will bring the tea and the knife, and
as he goes will nod casually towards a gigantic
sideboard not far away, and I shall understand.
The rest will be easy. It is possible, indeed
highly probable, that the two old women will
still be sitting there, but I do not imagine for
a moment that they will interfere or pay any
attention to my business with the knife and
the sideboard. They will, I fancy, just go on
whispering together, like true gentlefolk staying
at a quiet hotel.

THE ARTIST

I DO not think I have met a happier man these last twelve months than the artist I visited the other week. The thought of him keeps joggling through my mind like a pleasant tune. I called to see him because I happened to be near the Yorkshire dale in which he lives, and I wanted to buy a drawing or two from him. I had seen work of his in London, delightful little water-colours, like enchanted windows opening for me on the moors and fells, the grey humped bridges, the fantastically walled fields of Yorkshire. Water-colour is the medium that pleases me most, particularly in English landscape, where it gives, as nothing else can give, the soft radiance of our own country-side, the mild play of light and shade, the mingling of rain and sunshine, the misty meadows and the plum-bloom of the hills. If I lived as some of my friends do, exiled in some empty and baking place over the sea, I should never have the courage to possess a good water-colour of English country, for if I had it I should want to dive through the little window, back into the hawthorn shade or the glimmer of twilit fields. I admit that water-colours of

The Artist

this quality want—as people say—a bit of doing. Yet I know nothing that announces itself so clearly as a good water-colour, or perhaps I should say what seems to me a good water-colour. Such a one—and you can see the family likeness in all the good ones whether they were painted yesterday or a hundred and twenty years ago—seems as easy and happy as a shepherd's or a sailor's remark about the weather ; it is, indeed, just like that, a knowing and loving eye cocked at things ; and there is always weather in your good, true water-colour, for though it appears the simplest but deftest little pattern of light and shade, the moment's play of colour caught and fixed for ever by a miracle of pigment and camel-hair and water, just a few washes on a bit of paper, yet looking at it you know at once what it would feel like to be walking there and the very smell of the place is in your nostrils. But this—you will understand—is not art criticism, which I leave to persons more sensitive and learned.

Well, I liked the man's work, felt sure I should like him, and so I paid my call, climbing up from one dale, losing myself in the clouds for half an hour or so, and then descending into another lovely long green valley, filled with limestone cliffs, bare slopes, and tiny grey villages, in which the cottages were huddled together like sheep in winter and for the very same reason. In this dale, in a bungalow perched on the hillside, I found him. He was the very man I expected him to be, and that fact alone made me happy, not because it flattered my judgment, but because it seemed to steady life, give it a shape and purpose for once. There are times when we are weary of piquancy, odd contrasts, the unexpected, when we are not pleased to find once more that the admired poet looks and talks like a butcher; thus I was glad to see that the artist resembled the man I had imagined behind his pictures. He was not, of course, a bearded, velvet-jacketed creature. No water-colourist, tramping and bicycling scores of miles over the Pennines every week, could possibly look like that. My man was bluff and weathered, a robust middle-aged fellow, with a shock of greying curly hair, a round red face, little dancing eyes, with a homely accent that had vowels as broad as the Yorkshire acres. His wife, who was small and round and excitable, ready to set out tea and scones or talk about pictures and places or pack a little bag for a journey to Samarkand first thing in the morning, was the very Eve for this large simple Adam, and it was easy to see that they had been the closest of companions for twenty years or so and that they were very happy together.

He had, I believe, been in business for many years and must have been past forty when he decided (and I can imagine the two of them

The Artist

talking it over many and many a night) to
leave his office or little warehouse for ever and
turn professional artist. They were childless
people, whose wants were few, and it would
not be difficult for them to live on very little.
To this day, I do not suppose it costs the two
of them more than about three pounds a week
in all, when they are living in their bungalow.
Two or three times a year, however, they set
out on their travels, to give him a change of
painting country, and they talk of these places
they visit, it might be Wells or Whitby, as you
might talk of Bucharest or Baku, and as they
talk you can see them walking together down
these distant streets, him with his book and
box and little curved pipe and the wife trotting
briskly by his side and missing nothing, having
all manner of tiny adventures.

He is beginning to sell his work now, and
like a sensible man he prefers to sell what he
can in his own studio and not through dealers,
who will charge twenty-five guineas sometimes
for what he himself will let you have for five.
(By the way, artists ought to set up co-operative
shops in all the large towns, shops in which
their work is always displayed and can be
bought at a reasonable price. Shops are much
better than exhibitions. If all the people who
have between five hundred and two thousand
pounds a year could be persuaded into becoming
art patrons, if only to the extent of ten or

fifteen guineas a year, what a difference it would make ! The trouble is that art is treated as if it were a rich man's plaything, and the artists themselves are partly to blame.) Well, he pulled out drawers and unfastened port-folios and so produced dozens and dozens of drawings, shaking his head over some, smiling at others, occasionally muttering something about ' a nice tone ', and for ever kept on lighting his little curved pipe. Meanwhile, we passed through agonies of indecision, and enjoyed ourselves immensely. There was an interval too during which we all retired to a delightful veranda, covered in with glass, which faced the broad valley and showed us a pageant of sunlight and cloud and woods and distant moorland ; and there we drank tea and ate scones and listened to the wind shouting down the dale. I have always longed for a veranda or balcony, one that looked out upon either the sea or some North-country landscape, for a man in such a place feels sheltered and at home and is yet able to let his spirit go roaming ; he is at once on his own hearth and yet over the hills and far away.

Much as I enjoyed the work I saw there, work so honest and sane and yet sensitive, delicate, I enjoyed the artist himself still more. He seemed to me one of those rarest of creatures, a happy man. Many people, of course, reach a kind of contentment, but frequently it is

The Artist

simply because they are rather piggy. But this man was anything but piggy, and he was clearly living in the spirit just as he was living in the flesh. He had found the work he wanted to do, and he was happy doing it. At times, of course, he must be dissatisfied with himself, but never, I think, radically dissatisfied, never touching anything that could be called despair, only feeling that the last two or three drawings were bad and that he must really try to do better.

He had nothing of that restless and insatiable vanity which is the curse of the artistic life, which sometimes annoys me so much that I want to denounce myself and most of my fellow-writers as a set of performing monkeys. There are times when I feel that the literary life is really and truly a dog's life, since it consists so largely in jumping about and barking and asking for a pat on the head. Much should be forgiven us, however, because of our dreary and unnatural occupation, which keeps us indoors churning away our thoughts and fancies, and lacks bustle and chat and a cheerful activity of the body. The artist, on the other hand, is not only able to create, but he is also able to potter, and there is health for him in the quick little movements of his hands. Moreover, he is in a better position than the writer to estimate the worth of what he is doing. In addition, if he is a water-colourist and a landscape man, his

work takes him out into the open, on to the
moors, down through the woods, to the bridge
or the church or the old mill, and he can let
the sun and wind and rain cleanse him of all
sick fancies ; he can enjoy the whole spread
and bloom of things without feeling that he is
idling. And if he has to think, it is only
thought directed to one certain end ; his
material is not thought ; so that he is at
liberty to think for fun or not think at all, just
as he pleases. His art is such that he may
remain as simple as a child and yet create fine
work ; and, indeed, I cannot help feeling that
water-colour demands a simple, unsophisticated
soul, filled with happy wonder and content to
mirror the beauty of the world, without asking
questions and tormenting itself ; it is a form
of art that might have come out of Eden, and
perhaps has never left it.

The modern consciousness is compelled to
seek other mediums, and water-colours, like
lilting songs and tunes, are not in the movement. My acquaintance the artist is clearly
whole worlds away from the movement ; he
and his little curved pipe and his homely speech
and his water-colours with ' a nice tone ' and
his Carlyle and Ruskin and old romances and his
smiling wife and his happy simplicity are really
anachronisms ; he is only just such another as
David Cox, dead these seventy years ; and it
is obvious that in the rapid progress of thought

The Artist

and art and life, he has been left far behind.
But I cannot help thinking that he seems to
have been left in a better place than the one
they appear to be heading for, in a place where
it is possible to be innocent and industrious
and happy.

OUR THEATRE

OUR village is in a state of great excitement this week. Madame Such-and-Such ' and her Company of Talented Artistes from London ' —I quote the bills—are paying us their annual visit. They have taken over that large brick hut on the right near the church, our village recreation hall, famous for its dances and whist-drives. You can seat—that is, if you are Madame Such-and-Such and know all about these things—nearly two hundred people in our recreation hut, and what with chairs, forms with backs, forms without backs, and standing space, you can have a fine range of variety of prices, from 6d. to 2s.

Madame has put up a proper stage, curtain and all. I don't say it is a very big stage, for I imagine a horse would completely fill it ; nor do I pretend that the lighting arrangements are good, seeing that there are no footlights and that more light falls upon the first two rows of seats (as I know to my cost) than it does upon the stage ; nor do I think it altogether wise to smother one section of the orchestra (the piano and violin) behind a curtain on one side and to smother the other section (a drum) behind a

curtain on the other side ; and indeed it would
be easy to point out all manner of defects.
Nevertheless, it is a real stage, echoing to the
tread of real actors, and as it is the only one
we have here, we are glad to make the most
of it. Madame's spokesman before the curtain
told us last night that she expected all her old
friends and patrons to rally round her, and I
am sure she will not be disappointed. Full
houses should be the rule, for whole busloads
of playgoers will be coming in to our village,
from as far as Little Combe and Long Chumpton.
And there is, you must understand, an entire
change of programme every night, a different
four- or five-act play, different 'varieties', and
a different 'screaming sketch to conclude',
every night. Here is the old generosity, real
money's worth : play, variety, farce.

Moreover, as the man told us last night, all
the plays are of different kinds. On Wednesday
we are to have a piece that is a companion play
to the *Prisoner of Zenda* and 'hin the hopinion
of many dramatic critics a far superherior
play '. On Thursday we shall have the laugh-
able comedy *Which Is Which*, not to be con-
founded, we were told, with the comedy *Who's
Who* played here the last time the company
came ; and all those of us ' who desire a hearty
laugh ' are requested to attend on Thursday.
Friday gives us a fine drama of military life ;
and then, to crown the week, there will be

' that grand Saturday night drama of love and
hate '—*The Gipsy's Revenge*. I am looking
forward to *The Gipsy's Revenge*.

Last night, the opening performance of the
season, we had *The Village Vagabond*, played
to a crowded and enthusiastic house. I was
there myself and so know all about it. Who,
do you imagine, took our money at the door ?
If you think it was some hireling, then you are
very simple. Madame herself, already made
up for the part of Mother, took our money, and
gave us tickets and change with gestures that
showed she had not played the noble matron
for forty years for nothing. Madame takes the
money herself and, before she sweeps on to the
stage as the harassed wife and loving mother,
you may be sure she counts it too. Madame
has been in this business for a great many years.
Who showed me to my seat ? The very man
who, a quarter of an hour later, came on as
Jack, the wicked brother, the dissipated fop,
the spendthrift, forger, the would-be murderer
of his father. In the part, however, he wore
little black sidewhiskers that contrasted rather
piquantly with his brown hair, and proved that
he was no longer the gentleman who showed us
to our seats, but a scoundrel, a hissing plotter.

The Village Vagabond is none of your new
trumped-up melodramas. Crummles himself
must have opened with it many a time. It is
a melodrama in the real old tradition. That

Our Theatre

tradition decrees that as soon as a character is mentioned, somebody must look off and cry ' But here he comes ', that nobody must ever really go more than a few yards away from the scene so as to be ready to pop in again in a minute or two, that all the virtuous characters must be extremely sententious and rather silly and all the wicked ones very rude and even sillier. These pieces reveal to us the affairs of some planet quite different from this, one in which all the people who know one another meet at every turn and everybody is slightly mad but gloriously rhetorical. Not that we villagers mind that : we see enough of this world and are delighted to find ourselves in another one, strangely different, for an hour or two.

We liked these people, no matter how queerly they behaved. We liked Harry, the so-called village vagabond, really a fellow with a heart of gold, idolized by all the fisherfolk. He had very curly hair, wore a blue jersey and high boots, always talked very nobly at the top of his voice, and was always on hand to snatch at horsewhips and revolvers. We knew very well that he had never attempted to murder his father, that he had returned to the old home, from which he had been banished, merely to change his clothes, the clothes that he actually brought with him to the old home—a queer procedure certainly but not to be confused

with attempted murder. We knew that he
would escape from Portland, though we actually
saw him (and all the other characters too) in
the quarry there, slaving away putting two half
bricks in a bucket and then taking them out
again. And because we liked the comic Jew
moneylender, who called everybody ' Ma tear '
and had a passion for crawling about on all
fours, we knew that he too, though no better
than he should be, would escape, and be just
in time to give evidence, to point to the man
' who struck down his father in his brother's
clothes '. If you imagine that Father wore his
brother's clothes, you do not understand the
plot, though I must confess that the phrase
just quoted—Acts Three and Four were peppered with it—does suggest something of the
kind.

Jack, the bad brother, was rather too
mysterious a figure for my taste. Every time
he entered, you began asking yourself all
manner of puzzling questions. True, he was a
swell, almost a London swell—everybody said
so—and no doubt these swells are very different
from the rest of us. But why did he wear
white spats in the evening, with his dinner
jacket ? Was it to suggest that he had now
completely abandoned himself to a life of luxury.
And then why, later that evening, did he
exchange his dinner jacket for a morning coat,
still wearing his dress shirt and waistcoat, and

why was it somebody else's morning coat five sizes too large for him ? Why did he arrive in the Portland quarries dressed for tennis, with an open shirt and a blazer, yet wearing a straw hat and carrying a walking stick ? Was it so that he might all the more effectively mock at his wretched brother, now a convict in a grey flannel suit with broad arrows chalked on, and doomed to pick up half bricks ? Can you wonder that Ny-omi, his cousin and the heroine, should scorn his attentions and give her hand and heart to his brother, a man who asked for nothing more than a blue jersey and top boots and detested all sartorial profligacy and perversity ? Ny-omi was good. She took us back to the time when heroines were not thin sneering little creatures but fourteen stone of feminine sweetness and virtue, coming on with their sunbonnets and baskets, talking at all critical moments in the paragraphs of eighteenth century orators, and with rings left them by their mothers to give to the men who had won their hearts. To hear Ny-omi talk, as she did very frequently during those dark hours in the Portland quarries, of ' Heaven'sss helppp ', was to know that all would be well.

But Father and Mother were best of all. Father, so rich and hard-hearted, was the most worried-looking man I have ever seen : his face was all red lines. He wore a collar so very stiff and tall that he had not the heart to change it throughout the piece, not even when he came on, in the quarries, pretending, behind a beard and a peaked cap, to be a warder. He worked very hard during that act, for he came on twice as Father, in an astonishing top hat and frock coat, and twice or three times as a warder. Moreover, he used a colossal amount of breath in the delivery of his lines, for he put an ' h ' in the middle of every word and an ' a ' at the end. 'Tre-hewa, tre-hewa,' he would say, when for once he agreed with anybody ; or ' Ger-hoa yer-hewa hara ner-hoa ler-honger a ser-huna of mer-hine-a.' It reads queerly, I know, but it sounded magnificent.

Mother—Madame herself—was better still. She had not a great deal to do, but a moment of her was worth an hour of anybody else. Even Father seemed a mere mumbling modern compared with her ; she carried us back to the glorious antiquity of melodrama ; she was the noblest Roman of them all. Speech was beneath her ; she fairly sang her lines ; and with a few higher notes would have plunged us into oratorio. To hear her cry ' He is our son, spar-a-re himmm ! ' was to understand the grand manner ; you caught a glimpse of the stage when it *was* the stage. What a noble tragic figure she made in the Second Act, when the storm was raging as hard as the man with the whistle and drum could make it rage, and she was told to leave the house by Father ;

when she stood there with the good Harry's
coat flung over her ample bare shoulders, or
over part of them—for it was pitifully inade-
quate ; when lightning more terrible than that
of the storm flashed from her eyes, and in chest
notes deeper than the thunder she revealed the
strength and majesty of maternal love ! When
she swept out, you could have sworn that the
black night had really swallowed her ; it was
absurd to think that she was behind that little
curtain, having a nip of something and keeping
her eye on the takings. If her patrons do not
rally round her (and I can promise for one),
then the Drama is dead.

THE MAN WITH THE FLARE

IT was the flare I noticed first. It was lying beside a bundle of painted canvas and short poles on the station platform at Banbury. Had it been the usual paraffin flare (and by ' flare ' I mean those crude lamps that seem to be simply a canister of oil with a long spout), so much dingy metal, it would probably have been merged into the background of the station. I might not have noticed it at all ; and even if I had, I should probably have taken no interest in it. A dirty and oily flare would only have suggested the drab chaffering of little market-places, and I should have thought no more about it. But this flare was painted a bright orange, and was easily the most conspicuous and the most cheerful object on Banbury platform. It looked like a symbol of jovial and picturesque vagabondage, and stood out from the mass of luggage as a John drawing of a gipsy woman stands out in a room full of sedate landscapes. I kept my eye on it and waited for the owner to appear. The bundle at its side was obviously a little stall, the kind of stall at which you are offered a watch or half-a-crown if you perform some

216

The Man with the Flare

quite impossible feat with disks or a swinging
ball.

Presently the owner arrived, carrying a black
wooden box that apparently contained whatever
else he possessed. The man was worthy of his
flare. He was a shortish nippy fellow, wearing
a scarf of the same bright orange as his flare :
it relieved him from the necessity of carrying
collars and ties and studs and also it proclaimed
a challenge to life. His suit and his big cap
were faded, but I caught a glimpse, as he fussed
about with his box and bundle, of a red round
face that was even more lively than the scarf.
When the North-bound train came in, he saw
his flare and stall into the van and took himself
and his black box into an empty smoker. I
followed him, and tried to read my papers while
he brought out needle and thread from his box
and did a little mending ; but the very sight
of him made the papers seem duller and sillier
than ever, and I waited for him to speak.

It was not long before we were in talk, and
we yarned away—or rather, he yarned and I
listened—across some hundred and fifty miles
of English country and in several refreshment
rooms of Midland junctions over hurried bottles
of Bass. It is impossible to capture him and
pin him to a sheet of paper. You have to hear
his voice, so eloquent and yet so rusty (he had
been talking at the top of it for years, drowning
the neighbouring steam organs and sirens : he

15

was good at the ' patter ', he told me, and I
could well believe it), with its twang of the
fair-ground and the barrack-room and the
boxing-booth and its faint Scots burr. You
have to see his dancing black eyes for ever
punctuating his remarks with winks, and the
gestures that amply illustrated his recital,
whether it was a matter of taking a drink or
winning a light-weight championship. You
have to feel his nudges, for he was given to
stressing a point with his elbow. His winks
and nudges took you into his confidence, showed
you that whatever was being said was between
the two of you : his voice had taken the whole
world into its confidence for so long that now
it could not confine itself to one listener, so
that the winks and nudges had to be called in
as allies.

He was nothing if not dramatic, and he could
people a railway carriage or a refreshment room
with soldiers and boxers and showmen and
crowds. If he talked (as he did) of a friend of
his who ought to have been world's champion
at some weight or other—' Fight anybody.
Beat the Dixie Kid. Beat Birmingham Jack.
Beat the Fighting Fireman. Beat 'em all.
Fight anybody. But a fool, a mug. Do it for
nothing. Never got in with the click [the
clique] '—you really saw this man going about
and fighting anybody and beating everybody,
a whole epic of disinterested pugilism reeled

The Man with the Flare

through your mind. What is impossible to capture—unless he were displayed at great length—is the immense liveliness of him, that quality which made the commercial travellers and workmen who travelled with us seem by comparison the drabbest figures, men made out of wood.

He was a wandering Scot, one of five brothers. (I can tell you about them : one was killed in the war ; one is a bricklayer, earning seventy-five dollars a week somewhere in Mass., U.S.A. ; one is a donkey-man on a trawler ; and the other is the mate of a collier). Years ago, he had been in the militia and then he became a professional boxer, a light-weight, and he had a good deal to say about boxing. He was running a booth just before the war, but he joined up at once and got a bullet wound at Neuve Chapelle. (We talked war, of course, and found that our respective divisions had been neighbours, that we knew the same trenches and had been billeted in the same flour-mill). Since the war he had travelled the length and breadth of England, Scotland, Wales and Ireland, and—as he put it—all the islands too, ' Isle o' Lewis, Isle o' Arran, Isle o' Man, Anglesey, Isle o' Wight, Channel Islands (first time I landed in Jersey with fourpence, four pennies. Second time, with a hundred and four pounds, hundred and four) ', and had even worked his way through France and Belgium, sometimes with a boxing booth, sometimes as a quack doctor, sometimes with a 'Try Your Skill' stall. He and O. Henry's 'Gentle Grafter'—wasn't it Jeff Peters?—would have been comrades-in-arms in two minutes. His various adventures were merely hinted at in the course of conversation. Thus, talking of negroes, he would say: 'Very good fellers, some of 'em. There was So-and-so, came from Plymouth. Went round Devon and Cornwall and Somerset with him. Made him into a wild man. I'd say "Walla-Willa-Walla" and he'd say "Willa-Walla-Willa", and I'd tell 'em we were talking in his own lingo. Marvellous, isn't it?' And there was another negro, from Manchester, he had with him once in a boxing booth: 'Nice quiet feller. Died o' consumption. Fight anybody for three rounds, just three rounds, no more. Quid to anybody who could stand up to him for three rounds. Couldn't do any more. Been a great fighter if he could have stood it. Died o' consumption.'

At present he is running a ball on a string game, but does not think much of it. 'I'm in the wrong line,' he said. 'Not enough money about. You've got to sell 'em something. Feller I was stopping with last night, pal o' mine, is coining it. Sells rubber dolls. Ninepence in the shilling profit. Took a hundred and fifty quid in three days, a hundred and fifty. Spends it all. Tarts, booze, gives it

The Man with the Flare

away—good feller. Always has stock, though. Hundreds o' quids worth, stock, see it piled up in a corner of the caravan. Rubber dolls. That's the game. Sell 'em something.'

He travels for nine months out of the year —from fair to cattle-show, from regatta to race-meeting, meeting old pals at every turn, and then for three months, from January to March, I think, he goes back to his home in Scotland—' drinking beer and whusky.' Then he takes a free passage on his brother's collier to Sunderland, and begins all over again, with his little black box and his orange flare. He had no overcoat, which is probably the test of the real vagabond. I asked him where he stayed. 'Anywhere,' he said. 'Always get in somewhere. Don't bother much about eating. Can't eat breakfast—too much booze. Eat at the stalls—whelks—good for you, you know—chips and fish—anything. I'm all right.' And he looked all right, too, ruddy and brisk and twinkling.

He had a craftsman's delight in the tricks of the trade, and told me a hundred and one stories illustrating them. Here is one of them, though I cannot possibly reproduce his manner of telling it. 'Cleverest thing I ever saw or one of 'em,' he began, ' was at Such-a-place. D'you know it? Well, there's a race-meeting there, not much of one, farmers' meeting. I'm here with my stall, next to me is the boozing tent, and next to that there's a crowd running the three-card trick. They've one dressed as a parson, another as a farmer, and another as an old woman. They're just getting going when up comes a plain-clothes man, 'tec. He looks them over.' And he gave me an imitation of a plain-clothes man looking them over. 'This 'tec raises his hand, to beckon to two policemen. But the feller running the game clips him under the jaw and down he goes. The old woman falls on top of him, screaming. They all start shouting: 'Leave her alone!'' "He's drunk!" "Old enough to be your mother!" "Shame!" All the click's shouting away. In a minute the crowd's so thick the coppers can't get through. All the crowd's shouting now. The feller running the game pulls the old woman away, and them and the rest of the click slip to the back while the crowd's shouting at the 'tec and the coppers are pushing their way through. "He's drunk. Lock him up" and they get hold of him, and it takes them a minute or two to find out who he is. Clever, wasn't it? Never saw anything neater. All got clean away. Marvellous!'

His flow of talk uncovered for me a whole parasitic underworld of which you and I have only obtained odd glimpses, a world of fairs and little race-meetings and boxing booths and low pubs, of cheapjackery and pugilism, of 'tarts and booze'. It was as if he held that

The Man with the Flare

paraffin flare of his to the face of another England. Yet it was better talk than I hear in most places, and not only because it was more picturesque and dramatic, more full of the sap and savour of life, Hogarth and Morland instead of the artists of the magazine covers, but also because it had more genuine sense and sensibility, more downright humanity, whether he was talking of the war or Ireland or Communism or Capitalism, poor men and rich men, rascals and good fellows, drink and fighting and comradeship and death, than you are likely to discover in the talk of fifteen hundred railway carriages stuffed with newspaper-made opinions. The little man may not have seen life steadily and seen it whole by the light of his orange flare, but he had at least taken a good look at it for himself ; and I think Henry Fielding, after wagging a finger at him in the dock for being a vagabond and something of a cony-catcher, would have given him a slap on the back and a guinea afterwards. Just before we parted, he discovered that I 'wrote for the papers '. This excited him : 'I've got a fine subject for an article for you,' he cried. I was all curiosity. 'The cultivation o' the tomato in the Channel Islands,' he went on. 'There's a subject for you. The tomato. Marvellous.' He left me marvelling.

ALL THE NEWS

MOST of my childhood and my youth were passed in the suburb of a northern manufacturing town, and to that suburb I returned last week to spend a few days with some relatives. As we sat in the drawing-room, looking out through the window at the dark and dripping weather, the drifts of dead sycamore leaves, the passers-by hurrying through the rain, I asked for and was given all the news.

Some of it I could discover for myself as I stared out of the window. When I was a boy, this house was one of the first to be built at this edge of the town, and I remember the time when we looked out upon fields. Then the builder came both at the back and the front of us, and brought with him those triangular scaffoldings of thin planks that we boys promptly transformed into ships and caves. I think we rather welcomed the builder, for when his houses were only half erected, there were fine dangerous games to be played on his skeleton first-floors, running along the naked beams and chasing one another down the rough stairs. And there was one field at the back left untouched, and there, during the holidays, we played football, not merely for an hour or two but all day. The neighbourhood swarmed with boys then, and we were able to 'pick sides' about ten in the morning and keep the game going until dark, because we all had dinner and tea at different times and so simply ran home, bolted our food, and then hurried back to find the game still in progress. Homer might have found a theme in that football. Across the road, to the right, there was a large house and estate that had fallen in the hands of speculative builders, and for a year or so it furnished us with a paradise of play. There were vast shrubberies of laurel and rhododendron that turned you into Robin Hood or Little John at sight; a tiny lake that we contrived to navigate with a fearsome raft; and a mysterious long underground passage, about three feet high, down which an enterprising boy could crawl to his heart's content. To this day, when I think of those few acres of neglected garden, they seem richer and more enchanting than the whole of Brazil—Amazon, jungle, and all.

Now there are rows and rows of houses where once we played. Where our raft once lurched dubiously into the little lake, merchants and cashiers (perhaps the very boys I knew) tune in to Daventry, carve roast mutton, and bid three hearts. Further up the road, where you had but to take a turn to see the moors towering

distantly to the skies, there are villas past the
counting and shops and garages, and fat motor-
buses go wheezing and groaning up and down
all day and half the night. The suburb sprawls
on for another mile at least, unhaunted by
those thirty fields—still bright with buttercups
in my memory—that it has murdered. It is
pleasant enough, and there is probably not a
house there in which I could not make a friend,
yet I hate the thought of this greedy monster
of brick-and-mortar eating and eating away at
the green hillsides. I feel like knocking at
every door and then crying to the opener :
' Why have you brought your little villa here ?
Why have you stripped my old world of its
fields ? Why should this suburb exist at all ?
Who are you, and who are your neighbours ?
What are you all doing ? ' I can understand
the exasperation of such a one as Mr. H. G.
Wells, who has long demanded of his fellow-
citizens that they should justify their existence.
He must have fallen into the mood, years ago,
when he visited the haunts of his youth and
found a monstrous new suburb in place of the
old smiling fields.

Well, we sat in the drawing-room, staring out
at the dead leaves and the wet pavement, and
I heard all the news. A face would come
floating across the lighted screen of memory, a
name would start up from nowhere, and I would
ask, ' What's become of So-and-so ? ' Then

they would reflect and consult one another, and after a minute or two I would have the news. It was, on the whole, the very stuff of melancholy. Sometimes we laughed, sometimes indeed we rocked with laughter, being touched with the humour that has tears for its neighbour and companion ; but the tale of life that came out, so stammering and episodic and unfinished, was not one of those wholesome and happy fictions for which the editors of magazines, who apparently know life and will have none of it, have such a passion. What had become of the commercial traveller with the rolling walk ? Ah, he became very strange in his manner, very strange, and at last they had to take him away, and he's in an asylum now. Yes, that's his wife going down now ; very sad for her ; she's having to let rooms, just keeps going. And the plump little man who played the violin ? Still alive, but his wife is paralysed all down one side, never goes out. What happened to the Such-and-such family, that jolly teasing crowd ? The father went bankrupt, and they had to sell up and move into a little house at the other side of the town ; nobody at home now but the old people ; Ralph's gone off somewhere ; Hilda is in South Africa, married ; Harry's consumptive and has to keep going to Switzerland ; and Eric—the little funny one, you remember—was killed in the war. And old Doctor Mesworth, the

vegetarian and socialist ? Dead, long since :
his wife and daughter left him, and then one
day they found him dead in his room ; he had
been queer for some time. Yes, wasn't he
funny ! We laugh a little at the thought of
him, with his shock of grey hair, his booming
voice, his tactlessness, his innocent enthusiasms ;
but I wish I did not have a little image of him
dying in that room. It is not death but the
thought of that last spell of life, when he was
alone, neglected, with all things greying and
chilling for him, that hurts me somewhere at
the back of my mind.

So it went on. This one—dead. That one
—disappeared. The others growing frail, taking
to their beds, mumbling in their talk, falling
into poverty, quarrelling with their wives and
husbands and children and friends. This was
the news as I heard it, and the time soon came
when I asked no more questions. Life was
jigging merrily on : boys were kicking footballs
somewhere ; girls were meeting their lovers ;
young men were being promoted ; youthful
married people were excitedly moving into
really convenient houses at last ; babies—
astonishing babies—were arriving from nowhere
to look, for a week or two, just like their fathers ;
friendships were being built up out of talk and
firelight ; happy families (if there are any left)
were cracking their little absurd jokes ; somebody was discovering Shelley all over again or

All the News

Mozart or Girtin or Cervantes; the moors were still there, facing the skies undaunted, with winds blowing over them that the town never knew, winds with the salt and blue magic of the Atlantic in them. All this I knew, but no intelligence of it came my way. Perhaps that was because I asked for the news, and such glimpses of happiness, as every reader of the daily prints must know, are no part of the news. And then my reporters themselves were looking at life from the western, the sunset slope of the hill. I too was to blame, for I could only ask about those people who were making their way out of the world and not those who were just coming into it. That is one reason why this news of life is so melancholy: we know the men and women who have died, whereas those who have been born are strangers to us; we must take our stand near the entrance to the graveyard, not where the infants go crowing in their perambulators.

Then, again, to return after years and gather all the news is to look down on life from a great height. It is seen as a tragedy with a few comic scenes thrust in here and there. There cannot be any happy endings in this world. That is why there is something depressing about biographies, which really should end when their subjects have reached some shining peak of prosperity. As it is, these chroniclers, with their drooping paragraphs, their mournful rhythms, go on and on, until at last the tale becomes a sad recital of lost friends and failing powers, loneliness and death, a tragedy but a tragedy meanly robbed of its blank verse, its roll of drums, its funeral cannon roaring over Elsinore. The old wife who tells her melancholy tale knows what life is. And why should I be so surprised, so hurt ? What did I expect ? What have the wisest always said of man in this world ? The truth is, I belong to a daft generation of romantic hedonists, who for some very obscure reason imagine that to live means to be happy, that joy is somewhere round the corner, and that if something or other were abolished we should all be happy daylong. Thus, you find us for ever hurt and screaming. ' Why am I not happy ? ' we cry in our little novels and plays. Why should we be happy ? Who gave us such false reports of this planet ? It would, I think, be doing a kindness to our children if we introduced them, at a very early age, to the views of such a one as Dr. Johnson, who saw this world as a vale of misery, and so never ran hurt and screaming when he heard all the news, but stoutly grasped and thankfully enjoyed every little cheerful thing that came his way. But it is too late to change the pattern of our own minds.

I need hardly say that I myself was never more cheerful and comfortable, thank you, being—you may say—well out of the news.

All the News

I am only t-t-t-t-tutting from an arm-chair just as I was when I heard about the Such-and-such family and old Doctor Mesworth. I am also wondering what, after all, *is* the pattern of my mind.

PRINTED BY
JARROLD AND SONS LTD,
NORWICH

METHUEN'S GENERAL LITERATURE

A SELECTION OF

MESSRS. METHUEN'S PUBLICATIONS

This Catalogue contains only a selection of the more important books published by Messrs. Methuen. A complete catalogue of their publications may be obtained on application.

ARMSTRONG (Anthony).

TWO LEGS AND FOUR. Illustrated by RENÉ BULL. 5s. net.
LIVESTOCK IN BARRACKS. Illustrated by E. H. SHEPARD. 6s. net.

WARRIORS AT EASE.	WARRIORS STILL AT EASE.
PERCIVAL AND I.	PERCIVAL AT PLAY.
HOW TO DO IT.	ME AND FRANCES.

Each 3s. 6d. net.

BAIN (F. W.).

IN THE GREAT GOD'S HAIR.	A DRAUGHT OF THE BLUE.
AN INCARNATION OF THE SNOW	A MINE OF FAULTS.
A DIGIT OF THE MOON.	THE LIVERY OF EVE.
A HEIFER OF THE DAWN.	AN ESSENCE OF THE DUSK.
THE DESCENT OF THE SUN.	THE ASHES OF A GOD.
BUBBLES OF THE FOAM.	A SYRUP OF THE BEES.

THE SUBSTANCE OF A DREAM.
Each 3s. 6d. net.

BELLOC (H.).

A HISTORY OF ENGLAND. In Five Volumes. Vols. I, II and III.
Each 15s. net.
MARIE ANTOINETTE. Illustrated. 18s. net.
PARIS. Illustrated. 8s. 6d. net.
THE PYRENEES. Illustrated. 8s. 6d. net.

ON NOTHING.	HILLS AND THE SEA.
ON SOMETHING.	FIRST AND LAST.
ON.	THIS AND THAT.
ON ANYTHING.	ON EVERYTHING.
EMMANUAL BURDEN.	A PICKED COMPANY.

Each 3s. 6d. net.

BIRMINGHAM (George A.).

A WAYFARER IN HUNGARY. Illustrated. 8s. 6d. net.
SPILLIKINS.   SHIPS AND SEALING-WAX.
Two Volumes of Essays. Each 3s. 6d. net.

2

CHESTERTON (G. K.).

COME TO THINK OF IT . . . 6s. net.
G. K. C. AS M.C. Edited by J. P. DE FONSEKA. 7s. 6d. net.

GENERALLY SPEAKING.	CHARLES DICKENS.
THE OUTLINE OF SANITY.	ALL THINGS CONSIDERED.
TREMENDOUS TRIFLES.	FANCIES VERSUS FADS.
A MISCELLANY OF MEN.	THE FLYING INN.
ALARMS AND DISCURSIONS.	THE USES OF DIVERSITY.

THE BALLAD OF THE WHITE HORSE.

Each 3s. 6d. net.

WINE, WATER AND SONG. 1s. 6d. net.

EINSTEIN (Albert).

RELATIVITY : THE SPECIAL AND GENERAL THEORY. 5s. net.
SIDELIGHTS ON RELATIVITY. 3s. 6d. net.
THE MEANING OF RELATIVITY. 5s. net.
THE BROWNIAN MOVEMENT. 5s. net.

EISLER (Robert).

THE MESSIAH JESUS AND JOHN THE BAPTIST. According to Flavius
Josephus' recently rediscovered " Capture of Jerusalem " and the
other Jewish and Christian sources. Illustrated. £2 2s. net.

FIELD (G. C.).

MORAL THEORY : An Introduction to Ethics. 6s. net.
PLATO AND HIS CONTEMPORARIES. 12s. 6d. net.

FYLEMAN (Rose).

FAIRIES AND CHIMNEYS.	*Twenty-first Edition.*
THE FAIRY GREEN.	*Thirteenth Edition.*
THE FAIRY FLUTE.	*Tenth Edition.*

FAIRIES AND FRIENDS.	THE RAINBOW CAT.
FORTY GOOD-NIGHT TALES.	THE ADVENTURE CLUB.
FORTY GOOD-MORNING TALES.	TWENTY TEA-TIME TALES.

EIGHT LITTLE PLAYS FOR CHILDREN.
SEVEN LITTLE PLAYS FOR CHILDREN.

Each 3s. 6d. net.

THE DOLLS' HOUSE. Illustrated. 5s. net.
A GARLAND OF ROSE'S: Collected Poems. Illustrated. 8s. 6d. net.
GAY GO UP. Illustrated. 5s. net.
A PRINCESS COMES TO OUR TOWN. Illustrated. 5s. net.

GIBBON (Edward).

THE DECLINE AND FALL OF THE ROMAN EMPIRE. Edited, with Notes,
Appendixes, and Maps, by J. B. BURY. Illustrated. Seven Volumes.
Each 15s. net. Also, unillustrated. Seven Volumes. Each 7s. 6d. net.

GLOVER (T. R.).

THE CONFLICT OF RELIGIONS IN THE EARLY ROMAN EMPIRE. 10s. 6d.
net.
POETS AND PURITANS. 10s. 6d. net.
VIRGIL. 10s. 6d. net.
FROM PERICLES TO PHILIP. 12s. 6d. net.

GRAHAME (Kenneth).

THE WIND IN THE WILLOWS. *Thirty-sixth Edition.* 7s. 6d. net. **Also**
Pocket Edition, 3s. 6d. net. Leather, 7s. 6d. net. Also illustrated by
WYNDHAM PAYNE. 7s. 6d. net. *See also* Milne (A. A.).

HADFIELD (J. A.).

PSYCHOLOGY AND MORALS. 6s. net.

HALL (H. R.).

THE ANCIENT HISTORY OF THE NEAR EAST. Illustrated. £1 1s. net.
THE CIVILIZATION OF GREECE IN THE BRONZE AGE. Illustrated. £1 10s. net.
A SEASON'S WORK AT UR OF THE CHALDEES. Illustrated. £1 5s. net.

HEATON (Rose Henniker).

THE PERFECT HOSTESS. Decorated by ALFRED E. TAYLOR. 7s. 6d. net.
Also special de luxe edition, £1 1s. net.

HERBERT (A. P.).

TANTIVY TOWERS. 2s. 6d. net.
WISDOM FOR THE WISE. 5s. net.
HONEYBUBBLE & CO. 6s. net.
MISLEADING CASES IN THE COMMON LAW. 5s. net.
MORE MISLEADING CASES. 5s. net.
THE BOMBER GIPSY. 3s. 6d. net.
THE WHEREFORE AND THE WHY. Illustrated. 3s. 6d. net.
THE SECRET BATTLE. 3s. 6d. net.

HOLDSWORTH (Sir W. S.).

A HISTORY OF ENGLISH LAW. In Nine Volumes. £1 5s. net each.

HUTTON (Edward).

CITIES OF SICILY. Illustrated. 10s. 6d. net.
MILAN AND LOMBARDY.
THE CITIES OF ROMAGNA AND THE MARCHES.
SIENA AND SOUTHERN TUSCANY. NAPLES AND SOUTHERN ITALY.
                    Each illustrated '8s. 6d. net.
THE CITIES OF UMBRIA.   THE CITIES OF SPAIN.
VENICE AND VENETIA.   A WAYFARER IN UNKNOWN TUSCANY.
FLORENCE AND NORTHERN TUSCANY.   ROME.
COUNTRY WALKS ABOUT FLORENCE.
                    Each illustrated. 7s. 6d. net.

INGE (W. R.), Dean of St. Paul's.

CHRISTIAN MYSTICISM (The Bampton Lectures for 1899). 7s. 6d. net.

JOHNS (Rowland).

LET'S TALK OF DOGS.   ALL SORTS OF DOGS.
                    Each illustrated. 6s. net.
DOGS YOU'D LIKE TO MEET.   LET DOGS DELIGHT.
                    Each illustrated. 3s. 6d. net.
PUPPIES. Illustrated. 10s. 6d. net.

KENDRICK (T. D.).

A HISTORY OF THE VIKINGS. Illustrated. 18s. net.
THE AXE AGE. Illustrated. 6s. net.
THE DRUIDS. Illustrated. 12s. 6d. net.
THE ARCHAEOLOGY OF THE CHANNEL ISLANDS. Vol. I. The Bailiwick of Guernsey. Illustrated. £1 5s. net.

KIPLING (Rudyard).

BARRACK-ROOM BALLADS.	255th Thousand.
THE SEVEN SEAS.	186th Thousand.
THE FIVE NATIONS.	143rd Thousand.
DEPARTMENTAL DITTIES.	117th Thousand.
THE YEARS BETWEEN.	95th Thousand.

Four Editions of these famous volumes of poems are now issued, viz.:
Crown 8vo, Buckram, 7s. 6d. net. F'cap. 8vo, Cloth, 6s. net. Leather,
7s. 6d. net. Service Edition.—Two vols. each book. Square F'cap.
8vo. 3s. net each vol.; and 6s. net.
TWENTY POEMS. 486th Thousand. 1s. net.
A CHOICE OF SONGS. 2s. net.
A KIPLING ANTHOLOGY—VERSE. Cloth, 6s. net and 3s. 6d. net.
Leather, 7s. 6d. net.

KNOX (E. V.) (" Evoe ").

    THINGS THAT ANNOY ME.   PARODIES REGAINED.
                    Each 5s. net.
    THESE LIBERTIES. 4s. 6d. net.
    FANCY NOW !   HERE'S MISERY !
    QUAINT SPECIMENS.   FICTION AS SHE IS WROTE.
           MR. PUNCH ON THE LINKS.
                  Each 6s. net.
    AWFUL OCCASIONS.   GORGEOUS TIMES.
    IT OCCURS TO ME.   WONDERFUL OUTINGS.
             THIS OTHER EDEN.
             Each 3s. 6d. net.

LAMB (Charles and Mary).

    THE COMPLETE WORKS. Edited by E. V. LUCAS. Six Volumes. 6s.
    net each. The volumes are :
    1. MISCELLANEOUS PROSE.   3. BOOKS FOR CHILDREN.
    2. ELIA AND THE LAST ESSAYS   4. PLAYS AND POEMS.
        OF ELIA.   5 and 6. LETTERS.
    SELECTED LETTERS. Edited by G. T. CLAPTON. 3s. 6d. net.
    THE CHARLES LAMB DAY BOOK. Compiled by E. V. LUCAS. 6s. net.

LANKESTER (Sir Ray).

    SCIENCE FROM AN EASY CHAIR.
    SCIENCE FROM AN EASY CHAIR (Second Series).
    DIVERSIONS OF A NATURALIST.   GREAT AND SMALL THINGS.
             Each illustrated. 7s. 6d. net.
    SECRETS OF EARTH AND SEA. Illustrated. 8s. 6d. net.

LAUGHLIN (Clara E.).

    SO YOU'RE GOING TO GERMANY AND AUSTRIA !
    SO YOU'RE GOING TO SPAIN !   SO YOU'RE GOING TO FRANCE !
    SO YOU'RE GOING TO PARIS !   SO YOU'RE GOING TO ROME !
    SO YOU'RE GOING TO ITALY !   SO YOU'RE GOING TO ENGLAND !
             Each illustrated. 10s. 6d. net.
    WHERE IT ALL COMES TRUE IN ITALY AND SWITZERLAND. Illustrated.
    7s. 6d. net.

LINDRUM (Walter).

    BILLIARDS. Illustrated. 6s. net.

LODGE (Sir Oliver).

    MAN AND THE UNIVERSE. 7s. 6d. net and 3s. 6d. net.
    THE SURVIVAL OF MAN. 7s. 6d. net.
    RAYMOND. 10s. 6d. net.
    RAYMOND REVISED. 6s. net.
    MODERN PROBLEMS. 3s. 6d. net.
    REASON AND BELIEF. 3s. 6d. net.
    THE SUBSTANCE OF FAITH. 2s. net.
    RELATIVITY. 1s. net.
    CONVICTION OF SURVIVAL. 2s. net.

LUCAS (E. V.).

    THE LIFE OF CHARLES LAMB. Two Volumes. £1 1s. net.
    THE COLVINS AND THEIR FRIENDS. £1 1s. net.
    VERMEER THE MAGICAL. 5s. net.
    A WANDERER IN ROME. 10s. 6d. net.
    A WANDERER IN HOLLAND. 10s. 6d. net.
    A WANDERER IN LONDON. 10s. 6d. net.
    LONDON REVISITED (Revised). 10s. 6d. net.
    A WANDERER IN PARIS. 10s. 6d. net.
    A WANDERER IN FLORENCE. 10s. 6d. net.
    A WANDERER IN VENICE. 10s. 6d. net.
    A WANDERER AMONG PICTURES. 8s. 6d. net.

LUCAS (E. V.)—contd.

E. V. LUCAS's LONDON. £1 net.

THE OPEN ROAD. 6s. net. India Paper, Leather, 7s. 6d. net.
Illustrated by CLAUDE A. SHEPPERSON. 10s. 6d. net.

THE JOY OF LIFE. Cloth. 6s. net.
Leather, 7s. 6d. net. India Paper, Leather, 7s. 6d. net.

FIRESIDE AND SUNSHINE.	THE SECOND POST.
CHARACTER AND COMEDY.	GOOD COMPANY.
ONE DAY AND ANOTHER.	A FRONDED ISLE.
LOITERER's HARVEST.	OLD LAMPS FOR NEW.
EVENTS AND EMBROIDERIES.	LUCK OF THE YEAR.
THE GENTLEST ART.	A ROVER I WOULD BE.
GIVING AND RECEIVING.	HER INFINITE VARIETY.
ENCOUNTERS AND DIVERSIONS.	TURNING THINGS OVER.

Each 3s. 6d. net.

A BOSWELL OF BAGHDAD.	'TWIXT EAGLE AND DOVE.
THE PHANTOM JOURNAL.	ZIGZAGS IN FRANCE.
CLOUD AND SILVER.	TRAVELLER's LUCK.

Each 6s. net.

FRENCH LEAVES. Illustrated. 5s. net.

"THE MORE I SEE OF MEN . . ."	IF DOGS COULD WRITE.
OUT OF A CLEAR SKY.	" . . . AND SUCH SMALL DEER."

Each 3s. 6d. net.

THE PEKINESE NATIONAL ANTHEM. Illustrated. 1s. net.
See also Lamb (C. and M.)

LYND (Robert).

THE BLUE LION.	THE PEAL OF BELLS.
THE MONEY-BOX.	THE ORANGE TREE.
THE LITTLE ANGEL.	THE GOLDFISH.
THE GREEN MAN.	THE PLEASURES OF IGNORANCE.

Each 3s. 6d. net.

IT's A FINE WORLD. 5s. net.

McDOUGALL (William).

AN INTRODUCTION TO SOCIAL PSYCHOLOGY. 10s. 6d. net.
BODY AND MIND. 12s. 6d. net.
AN OUTLINE OF PSYCHOLOGY. 10s. 6d. net.
NATIONAL WELFARE AND DECAY. 6s. net.
ETHICS AND SOME MODERN WORLD PROBLEMS. 7s. 6d. net.
AN OUTLINE OF ABNORMAL PSYCHOLOGY. 15s. net.
CHARACTER AND THE CONDUCT OF LIFE. 10s. 6d. net.
MODERN MATERIALISM AND EMERGENT EVOLUTION. 7s. 6d. net.

MAETERLINCK (Maurice).

THE BLUE BIRD. 6s. net and 2s. 6d. net.
THE BETROTHAL. 6s. net and 3s. 6d. net.
DEATH. 3s. 6d. net.
OUR ETERNITY. 6s. net.
THE UNKNOWN GUEST. 6s. net.

MALLET (Sir C. E.).

A HISTORY OF THE UNIVERSITY OF OXFORD. Three Volumes. Illustrated. Each £1 1s. net.

MARLOWE (Christopher).

The Works of. In 6 Vols. General Editor, R. H. CASE.

I. LIFE OF MARLOWE; AND DIDO, QUEEN OF CARTHAGE. By C. F. TUCKER BROOKE. 8s. 6d. net.

II. TAMBURLAINE THE GREAT. By U. M. ELLIS-FERMOR. 10s. 6d. net.

III THE JEW OF MALTA and THE MASSACRE AT PARIS. By H. S. BENNETT. 10s. 6d. net

METHUEN (Sir A.).

AN ANTHOLOGY OF MODERN VERSE. 232*nd Thousand.*
SHAKESPEARE TO HARDY: An Anthology of English Lyrics. 28*th Thousand.*
Each, Cloth, 6s. net. Leather, 7s. 6d. net.

MILNE (A. A.).

THOSE WERE THE DAYS. 7s. 6d. net.
TOAD OF TOAD HALL. A Play from Kenneth Grahame's " THE WIND IN THE WILLOWS." 5s. net.
BY WAY OF INTRODUCTION. 6s. net.

NOT THAT IT MATTERS.	IF I MAY.
THE DAY'S PLAY.	THE HOLIDAY ROUND.
ONCE A WEEK.	THE SUNNY SIDE.

Each 3s. 6d. net.

WHEN WE WERE VERY YOUNG.	211*th Thousand.*
WINNIE-THE-POOH.	118*th Thousand.*
NOW WE ARE SIX.	119*th Thousand.*
THE HOUSE AT POOH CORNER.	105*th Thousand.*

Each illustrated by E. H. SHEPARD. 7s. 6d. net. Leather, 10s. 6d. net.
THE CHRISTOPHER ROBIN STORY BOOK. Illustrated by E. H. SHEPARD. 5s. net.
THE CHRISTOPHER ROBIN BIRTHDAY BOOK. Illustrated by E. H. SHEPARD. 3s. 6d. net.
FOR THE LUNCHEON INTERVAL. 1s. 6d. net.

MORTON (H. V.).

THE HEART OF LONDON. 35*th Thousand.* 3s. 6d. net. Also, Illustrated by L. Hummel. 6s. net.
THE SPELL OF LONDON. 25*th Thousand.* 3s. 6d. net.
THE NIGHTS OF LONDON. 18*th Thousand.* 3s. 6d. net.

IN SEARCH OF ENGLAND. 84*th Thousand.*
THE CALL OF ENGLAND. 36*th Thousand.*
IN SEARCH OF SCOTLAND. 106*th Thousand.*
IN SEARCH OF IRELAND. 40*th Thousand.*
Each illustrated. 7s. 6d. net.

PETRIE (Sir Flinders).

A HISTORY OF EGYPT. Illustrated. Six Volumes.
1. FROM THE IST TO XVITH DYNASTY (12s. net). 2. THE XVIITH AND XVIIITH DYNASTIES (9s. net). 3. XIXTH TO XXXTH DYNASTIES (12s. net). 4. PTOLEMAIC EGYPT. EDWYN BEVAN. (15s. net.) 5. EGYPT UNDER ROMAN RULE. J. G. MILNE. (12s. net.) 6. EGYPT IN THE MIDDLE AGES. STANLEY LANE-POOLE. (10s. net.)

RICHARDSON (T. D.).

MODERN FIGURE SKATING. Illustrated. 15s. net.

RUTTER (Frank).

EL GRECO. Illustrated. £1 10s. net.

SELLAR (W. C.) and YEATMAN (R. J.).

1066 AND ALL THAT. A comic history. Illustrated by JOHN REYNOLDS. 50*th Thousand.* 5s. net.

SOMERVELL (D. C.).

ENGLISH THOUGHT IN THE NINETEENTH CENTURY. 6s. net.

TILDEN (William T.).

THE ART OF LAWN TENNIS (Revised Edition).
SINGLES AND DOUBLES.
Each illustrated. 6s. net.
LAWN TENNIS FOR YOUNG PLAYERS.
LAWN TENNIS FOR CLUB PLAYERS.
LAWN TENNIS FOR MATCH PLAYERS.
Each illustrated. 2s. 6d. net.

TILDEN (William T.)—contd.
THE COMMON SENSE OF LAWN TENNIS.
MATCH PLAY AND THE SPIN OF THE BALL.
Each illustrated. 5s. net.
ME—THE HANDICAP. 5s. net.

UNDERHILL (Evelyn).
MYSTICISM. (Revised Edition.) 15s. net.
THE LIFE OF THE SPIRIT AND THE LIFE OF TO-DAY. 7s. 6d. net.
CONCERNING THE INNER LIFE. THE HOUSE OF THE SOUL.
Each 2s. net.
MAN AND THE SUPERNATURAL. 7s. 6d. net.

VARDON (Harry).
HOW TO PLAY GOLF. Illustrated. 19th Edition. 5s. net.
THE COMPLETE GOLFER. Illustrated. 21st Edition. 12s. 6d. net.

WARD (A. C.).
TWENTIETH-CENTURY LITERATURE. 5s. net.
THE NINETEEN-TWENTIES. 5s. net.

WILDE (Oscar).
THE WORKS OF OSCAR WILDE. Sixteen Volumes. Each 6s. 6d. net.
Some also 2s. 6d. net.
1. LORD ARTHUR SAVILE'S CRIME AND THE PORTRAIT OF MR. W. H.
2. THE DUCHESS OF PADUA. 3. POEMS. 4. LADY WINDERMERE'S FAN.
5. A WOMAN OF NO IMPORTANCE. 6. AN IDEAL HUSBAND. 7. THE
IMPORTANCE OF BEING EARNEST. 8. A HOUSE OF POMEGRANATES. 9.
INTENTIONS. 10. DE PROFUNDIS AND PRISON LETTERS. 11. ESSAYS.
12. SALOME, A FLORENTINE TRAGEDY, AND LA SAINTE COURTISANE.
14. SELECTED PROSE OF OSCAR WILDE. 15. ART AND DECORATION.
16. FOR LOVE OF THE KING: A Burmese Masque (5s. net). 17. VERA,
OR THE NIHILISTS.